# The Power of Epistles:

## A Series of Emails from Don Young to John and Eydie Jones

BY

## Don Young

**DORRANCE**
PUBLISHING CO
EST. 1920
PITTSBURGH, PENNSYLVANIA 15238

The contents of this work, including, but not limited to, the accuracy of events, people, and places depicted; opinions expressed; permission to use previously published materials included; and any advice given or actions advocated are solely the responsibility of the author, who assumes all liability for said work and indemnifies the publisher against any claims stemming from publication of the work.

Dorrance Publishing Co
585 Alpha Drive
Suite 103
Pittsburgh, PA 15238
Visit our website at *www.dorrancebookstore.com*

ISBN: 978-1-6491-3336-6
eISBN: 978-1-6491-3303-8

# ABOUT THE DAILY EMAIL

# FROM DON BELK YOUNG

# TO JOHN AND EYDIE JONES

## NOVEMBER 27, 2000-MARCH 14, 2001

With footnotes dated March 25, May 20, June 15, 2001

## TO THE READER

John and Eydie Jones have written an introduction to a series of daily emails that I began when they moved to Little Rock for some intensive (and extensive) medical procedures that Eydie was undergoing to deal with multiple myeloma. My intent in these missiles, which have now been termed epistles, was to try to provide, if only for a moment or two, a distraction from the worry of the day or the inevitable feeling of despair that comes with such a serious illness.

I did not plan to write each day, but after the first few days thought that it was a good thing to do. With this self-induced motivation to provide a daily respite for the Joneses, it became something that I looked forward to and was determined to "do something" each day as long as they were in Little Rock.

Much of the nonsense and meanderings, stream of consciousness, and just plain silliness was a byproduct of reporting on UAB basketball and news about mutual acquaintances. But the fun part was when something occurred to use while the fingers were on the keyboard and it "just happened...."

With apologies to all who subject themselves to perusal of this sophomoric silliness, I do believe that you might find a chuckle or two among The Epistles.

Finally, a word or two about missing words, incomplete sentences, punctuation lapses and any other technical errata. I take no responsibility and do not worry about it and you should do the same. To avoid perfection is to establish a sense of normality, don't you think?

Proceed with caution. We now deliquesce without being minacious.


DON BELK YOUNG
September 1, 2005

# THE POWER OF EPISTLES

The email messages that follow were a daily transmission from Don Young to John and Eydie Jones, beginning November 27, 2000, and continuing through March 14, 2001. We were in Little Rock during this time. We had closed our home in Birmingham and leased an apartment in Little Rock in order for Eydie to have a third bone marrow transplant at the Medical Center of The University of Arkansas.

In October 1995 Eydie was diagnosed with multiple myeloma, a very rare and incurable cancer that attacks the bone marrow and spreads throughout the body. The average lifetime was three years after diagnosis.

After much research and discussion we decided to go to Arkansas for this treatment; the first transplant was in July 1996, the second one in November 1996. Eydie was now in full remission and returned home and to work full time. During a scheduled follow up at Arkansas it was discovered that cancer cells were again in her bone marrow. After a year of returning to Little Rock every three months for a variety of unsuccessful treatments, Eydie was advised that her only remaining option was an allogenic transplant, in which stem cells are transplanted from a sibling. Her sister Janet was a perfect match.

We returned to Arkansas on Thanksgiving weekend in 2000. The most important piece of luggage we brought from home turned out to be our computer. It was a great source of keeping in touch with friends, family and Eydie's work colleagues. Eydie was admitted to the hospital on Dec. 2, 2000, for the allogenic transplant. She was an inpatient for six weeks followed by daily outpatient hospital visits until mid-March 2001. The success of this long-term treatment is that Eydie has a new immune system, a change of blood type, and is in complete remission.

The most enjoyable experiences that we had during our months away from home in 2000 and 2001 were the daily "Epistles" that showed up on our computer email screen. We named these messages "Epistles" because, to us during this time, they were like the Epistles from the Apostle Paul published throughout the New Testament, messages eagerly anticipated. They were a wonderful source of humor (most of the time) during non-humorous times and a welcome respite from the very serious health problems we were dealing with each day.

We want to extend our sincere thanks and greatest appreciation to Don Young for his efforts, time and thoughtfulness during these challenging days.

JOHN AND EYDIE JONES

# Contents

## JANUARY 1-31 2001

## March 1-June 16, 2001

# J Jones to Don Belk

# THE POWER OF EPISTLES:

## A SERIES OF EMAILS FROM DON YOUNG TO JOHN AND EYDIE JONES

## don belk young

**From:**          don young [donbelk@bellsouth.net]

**Sent:**          Monday, November 27, 2000 – 4:55P.M.

**To:**          john downey <jjones2742@aol.com>

**Subject:**          THE REAL NEWS

Let us start at the beginning.

A lot of silly stuff going on in Florida. Florida is a good place to do silly stuff. That has been imparted to me from an unimpeachable source and she cannot be bribed, either. I have been silly in Sarasota, of all places, not to mention Tamps and Miami Beach. Tallahassee was best of all; more about that when we have a bigger audience. We heard that the residents of Okaloosa County were a lot more interested in the weather than the election because it directly affects their livelihood—doing things to and for tourists. It has been reported from the usual unreliable sources that approximately 72.673% of the ordinary people had become extremely uninterested in who the President of the U.S. was going to be. When pressed for more detail comments, the respondents responded with 584 different answers (103 people in the survey so you can see that they had multiple conclusions). My conclusion that this can be a dangerous thing in our present state of totally dull everyday happenings.

A very uneventful day so far, and no reason to believe that we will have significant variations from that theme. We know that you have no interest at all in how long it takes to vacuum the upstairs carpet, won't bother you with that. But it takes longer than it would otherwise when you do it more than once. I would understand if you are becoming uncomfortable with this drivel unless I admit that it is indeed the most useless nonsense since _____ (fill in the blank since we cannot think of anything right now, having spent so much energy making a point of not bothering the little grey cells).

First, a shower and a shave, or is it the other way 'round. Has Yumyum (that's a cat) followed or still in bed with Woowoo. If the cat is in the bed, turn off stairway landing light, go downstairs, and turn off security alarm. (Once in awhile open the front door before turning off the alarm, then apologize profusely for being stupid enough to do that, but by then you have someone to talk to—talk about having a scintillating conversation. See if the coffee maker is set for 7:15. If not, ignore it because there must be a reason. Get a shot of prune juice—a great way to start the day because it makes the orange juice taste really good. Go outside to get the newspaper.

Well, it is a beginning. Please be assured that it will get better, starting tomorrow. So do not go away. A new beginning will begin to start tomorrow or as soon after as conditions permit.

everyone is ENTITLED to a struggle

## don belk young

**From:**          "don belk young" <donbelk©bellsouth.net>
**To:**             "john downey" <jiones2742@aol.com>
**Sent:**         Tuesday, November 28, 2000 3:00 PM

Well, it's the next day here. I assume that it is the next day in Fla. also, but can't tell it by the news. I seem to be hearing the same mind numbing nonsense that was being talked about yesterday. Yeah, I know that it is different people in many cases, but we are still trying to find the will of the people and uphold the rule of law. Do these objectives conflict.

Have already had a big day. WENT TO THE MAILBOX TWICE. First time for outgoing items (remembered to raise the flag); second time to pick up today's mail. Threw it all in the trash so felt like we were getting a fresh start.

—John, skip this paragraph—this is for Edith

Checked the email. Had a note from Mark about yelling Gore instead of Fore. This gives a golfer the privilege of putting the ball where it was supposed to go and the golfer can take as many swings as it takes to get the desired result. In a recent game in Palm Beach, FL, it took one golfer 19 days.

Then brought in the newspaper. It also had yesterday's news, but that is what it is supposed to do, so what is one to do. I have temporarily lost touch with my eruditiousness and am doing to use that as an excuse until it shows up again. If you determine that these notes are not tedious enough to induce a serious case of drowsiness, I can make a copy of some of my mother's "letters" in the 1970's. No hurry. Let me know anytime if you would like to have them.

OK. So the newspaper is now finished along with one cup of yesterday's coffee. We have a tradition that sort of says "if you have left over coffee, drink that while fresh coffee is being made." And it works great for me. Do you know why? Would you like to know? Just let me know if you do and I will think up something to say about that or something else. You may have discerned by now that I am in training for political office. I have discovered the basic premise of politalk. (That is a brief form for political talk and will be used in the future without explanation.) The basic premise of politalk is to always tell the questioner that he/she did not ask the right question so here is the answer to the question you meant to ask.

If you are getting excited just by reading this, just wait until you experience it for the first time. That reminds me, 1 meant to ask you whether you have had an epiphany. I heard that they are out there somewhere if you can just find one. And that they can be had by searching for them. You just have to believe. Please confirm if this your understanding of this phenomena. I have a tendency to be quite methodical, so please give directions in a straightforward one step at a time formula. Appreciate.

Again, if you think this is exciting, look for more in tomorrow's email.

11/28/2000

**don belk young**

| | |
|---|---|
| **From:** | "don belk young" <donbelk@bellsouth.net> |
| **To:** | "john downey" <jjones2742@aol.com> |
| **Sent:** | Wednesday, November 29, 2000 6:27 PM |
| **Subject:** | DAY THREE |

Well, this is truly a great day, Except for a dismal day trying to play golf in the rain—Roy Kirkpatrick and Bob Cummings were in my four-some—there was nothing that really had to be done except feed the cat, bring in the newspaper, make the coffee, and get some Grey Poupon mustard from Food World. So it is easy to see that it was what you could call a fun day.

So we have progressed to watching the TV coverage of today's news. And it seemed that the people reporting in Birmingham also noticed that we had rain in the morning and sunshine in the afternoon. All I did was throw some moldy bread on the lake and I really did not care whether the ducks or the swans or the turtles or the carp made a big deal of an unexpected meal. I tell you this is exciting stuff and it is a shame that everybody does not do the same thing every day. It would keep us from getting so excited about the possibility of counting 11,000,000 ballots. I think that is what 1 just heard. Must get back to trying to find out why my Achilles (please let me know how to pronounce that) tendon is so tender, commonly known as Achilles (there's that word again) tendonitis. This whole thing has serious ramifications for my golf game, which is about the 59th most important thing in my system of values right now.

OK. What happens after getting up, going through morning routine, playing golf in the rain, and making it through the day, we are now seriously discussing how to treat Yumyum royally and have not found a chad to let enough fight through to know what was the real intent of the chad or the cat, More about that later unless we forget to remember that we were going to solve that problem.

I hope you appreciate that these notes are original compositions and not some lame joke that has been retold x times. Tell you the truth, though, I would rather hear one of your old jokes than anything that has accosted these ears lately.

Looking at the above, I do not see a joke or any other kind of humor in there anywhere. So let me know if there is any.

It occurs to me that you do not yet know that we have a serious sense of humor here. Actually, we have been known to pretend to be amused when we were not. Never thought that we would write that out for all the world to see, but we are trying to keep up the pretension that everyday happenings that do not amount to a damn thing is important to somebody.

And if you do not like or appreciate the attitude that produces the kind of drivel that you have been subjected to for three days now, you can go to hell and please feed my hogs if I am unable to take care of them.

Be sure to read every word very carefully tomorrow. There may be something there that you/ need to know.

P.S. Visited with Jan and Ray Boothe for a few minutes last Saturday. Went by to get some basketball tickets so some of my relatives could see UAB win their first game of the season. I asked Jan whether she could stand up without falling down and she said NO. Otherwise Jan seemed to be just like she always was.

P.S.S. How about those Blazers. Hope you have a way of keeping up with UAB basketball while you are out of town, They are looking good!!!!!!!!!!

11/29/2000

DON YOUNG

## don belk young

| | |
|---|---|
| **From:** | "don belk young" <donbelk@bellsouth.net> |
| **To:** | "john downey" <jjones2742@aol.com> |
| **Sent:** | Thursday, November 30, 2000 11:09 AM |
| **Subject:** | ONE MORE TIME |

I believe that the time has come. Do not know what for or what about, but there has been a considerable lapse of time since the last event, so it is surely time.

As you can see from the above, it is not getting any better. But wait. There may be some semblance of sanity out there somewhere. You just have to look for it. I've heard about rocks only growing on the mossy side of a tree, so that may be the place to look.

Had a call from Dave Barry—well, it wasn't exactly a call, more like a mysterious message that just comes through the ozone somehow—anyhow, he said to cease and desist from these sorry imitations of serious nonsense, that he had patented silliness and mediocre journalism in the form of occasional essays about foibles. That's another thing I would like to be enlightened about. Just exactly what is a foible? Can you have more than one at the same time? Are they equally divided among the populace, or does the male population have all of them because of some genetic thing?

Speaking of exactly, have you noticed how that word is misused by everyone from President Elect Gore up to Jesse Jackson and his extreme right wing group when they are speaking about almost anything. A common expression is "We do not know just exactly what the answer is" when they really mean that they do not have the slightest clue and do not even understand the question. As that well known pundit whose initials are DBY would write—he cannot articulate very well—if you do not know the answer, apologize for being stupid, ignorant and uninformed, grovel a couple of times, and ask for enough machoism (is that a word) to engage in some politalk and just go on. Please go on. Please go a long ways gone.

A little more about the daily routine. We know that this is the part that you need to make a connection to reality on a daily basis. After the morning routine about the cat, the coffee, the newspaper, today's news bite, and a couple of phone calls, we are ready to look at the calendar to see what excitement awaits. And guess what Woowoo gets to meet her new doctor this afternoon. Then we get to go together to Lovoy's with a friend.

Had an exciting meeting at Hardee's to discuss bids for the lawn and shrub maintenance for our neighborhood homeowners association. Will not reveal any details unless you really want to know. Since you are learned (whoever is reading this) I will not be dilatory unless you want me to be because, in all humility, I do not know how to be learned or dilatory or humble.

One more thing. Have been trying to work in the word anathema but do not know enough about its meaning to use it in a nonsensical way so there it is.

Don't know about you, but that is about all I can stand so we will do more later (promise) and try to pick it up a notch.

In order to cancel this subscription you must submit a list of one or more dissatisfied (about anything) people or animals and certify by apologizing for such behavior in advance. You must know about feelings!!!

11/30/2000

## don belk young

| | |
|---|---|
| **From:** | "don belk young" <donbelk@bellsouth.net> |
| **To:** | "john downey" <jjones2742@aol.com> |
| **Sent:** | Friday, December 01, 2000 3:39 PM |
| **Subject:** | OLD RELIABLE STRIKES AGAIN |

Time marches on, and on and on and on. So today is Friday and the beginning of another month. You may not be interested at all in what we are doing or getting ready to do, but what it is the start of the weekend. We usually start a weekend sometime between awakening and making the coffee on Friday morning. But have been known to move it up or back or whatever you want to call it to midday Thursday or even Wednesday afternoon. One of the advantages of a careless, reckless lifestyle.

To continue to get you through one of our normal days—fist the cat, then the security system, then the coffee, then the newspaper, then the prune juice, (on Tuesday and Friday put out the trash and on Wednesday take out the recycle box), then see whether email has arrived and print out today's crossword puzzle. Go to the mailbox, throw away most of it, and make some totally unimportant comment about something. Do you think it possible to have a scintillating conversation in the middle of the day when nothing has happened except for discovery of a couple more dimples on punch card ballots in Florida. Well, you can. But we didn't.

Just noticed the truism posted on today's page on the calendar. It says, and I am not making this up, "Players who don't have consistent preshot routines consequently don't hit consistent shots." Just kind of grabs you by the, let's see, what does it grab you by, probably doesn't matter since you should have already been distracted by something on TV by now.

I challenge you once again to review the above very carefully to determine the existence of something meaningful. And please let me know if you make such a discovery so I can redouble my efforts to be more effective at not saying anything especially if it is written.

WARNING! If you print this from your computer, it will probably crash trying to find a virus that isn't there.

The daily routine stuff has never gotten much past the mailbox routine about noon or a little after. And you may not ever find out. I do not remember much about afternoons. And here is a partial list of events that give this result,

1. Not paying attention to what is going on.

2. Not giving a damn about what is going on.

3. Not enough memory capacity to remember what is going on.

4. If it happened yesterday, forget it.

5. Must not have been important. We've got a lot of that.

But surely you, being an adroit reader, can see through these excuses and figure out that the things you remember when you are sound asleep are called dreams and do not usually reflect reality, so you do not have a clue about what is going on.

No gnoig si tahw tuoba eulc a evah ton od ouy os. Read this backwards and you will know what has happened.

To reassure you one more time. It will get worse before it gets better. And that really is a promise.

Time to start the weekend. See ya!

12/01/2000

**don belk young**

---

| | |
|---|---|
| **From:** | "don belk young" <donbelk@bellsouth.net> |
| To | "john downey" <jjones2742@aol.com> |
| **Sent:** | Saturday, December 02, 2000 8:46 PM |
| **Subject:** | NEXT DAY |

Well, this is the next day after the start of the weekend. So the routine is a little different. No major variations, mind you, just enough to know that it is different. For example, in addition to getting gasoline for the car and picking up a prescription, went by McDonald's for an Egg McMuffin. That was for Woowoo. If you ever want to surprise her in a positive way, which is the best way, just have a stretch limo drive up with a waiter who delivers an Egg McMuffin. That will do it.

We were not surprised by the outcome of the Florida/Auburn game. Mark came by for the first half. And we suffered through the rest of the game. Topped It off with grilled pork chops, spinach and apple sauce.

Do you know why Tallahassee is the capital of Florida. We were at Lovoy's last evening and I made up a story to tell a young couple. It sounded so good that I will embellish it and make it more mundane than it has been so far. But it may take a full daily column to do that so you will have something to look for.

I have a question. You have experience as a coach, among other things. I do not remember hearing what your lifetime won/lost record is, so if you are embarrassed to talk about it, that's OK. But here is the question. Why does a coach—I have noticed that this occurs in football and basketball—push a player towards the field of action after he has a conversation with the player. The player is already turning to go to in as fast as he can and the coach pushes him into the fray. Why is this?

Remember. The lesson of Tallahassee is in your future.

12/02/2000

## don belk young

**From:** "don belk young" <donbelk@bellsouth.net>
**To:** "john downy" <jjones2742@aol.com>
**Sent:** Sunday, December 03, 2000 1:24 PM
**Subject:** HERE WE GO AGAIN


I just thought of something that I had never heard before. But it is a very revealing philosophy so would not be surprised if Apollo or Adonis or Adolph or Plato or Cato thought of it before but did not write it down because it is self-evident and surely occurs to each of us sometime. What I thought of was quote The more things change the more they stay the same. Since you have borderline qualifications as an erudite person, I expect that you had thought of it before but did not think it was a big deal. So left everyone else to think about it on their own time. But now I have got it and see no need to make a big deal out of it either.

We are thinking about you-all every day. And are praying for good things to happen for you and Eydie. We miss you and hope you get back soon when all is well.

Have you thought about the question regarding why a coach pushes a player into the game. it may be after a timeout or a substitution, but does not seem to occur when the game is starting. Would probably be too much to push all eleven football players at the same time. The germ of an idea about that is floating around out there somewhere. And intend to get one of the gray cells to work on it.

Today is another special day. Have not found out what is special-yet but it must be around somewhere. There was no news worth mentioning so will skip that. Have a piano recital to go to this afternoon. Desiree will play Jingle Bells for three minutes at the Galleria as part of Christmas at the mail.

More details about that after it takes place. Since she is a direct recipient of genes from the master. That was my great great grandfather—when they went through me they were in a dormant state but seem to have become extremely evident in each of my grandchildren. So far almost of them are perfect so it pleases me that the dormancy of the genes in certain generations did not diminish them. Perhaps I should get credit for not using any of the power of the genes. think about it.

Remember, the Tallahassee story will be in a future installment.

Woowoo and Yumyum are having a battle of wills today. I think it will be a tie.

12/03/2000

## don belk young

| | |
|---|---|
| **From:** | "don belk young" <donbelk@bellsouth.net> |
| **To:** | "john downey" <jjones2742@aol.com> |
| **Sent:** | Monday, December 04, 2000 8:27 PM |
| **Subject:** | AND YET ANOTHER |

Yes, this was a good day. It is not at all clear why that conclusion is justified but it seems to be OK. We are doing well after a bowl of butter beans and cornbread. And a little glass of wine. Not bad for a country boy. Of course Woowoo is a city girl and she thought it was pretty good.

I think that we are trying to have a winter season, but plan to meet the challenge and play golf in the morning. Gloria Moon told Woowoo that Jim has been to the golf course, new knee and all.

We went to Villa Rose again. They have a liquor license now so they were having a sort of celebration with drinks at half price. Anyhow we had a good time. Let's see, besides Woowoo, Judy was there and so was Shannon. Next thing we knew we agreed that it had been better than average although it was never mentioned. Interesting how the human mind can deal with complex social situations and never get into serious complicated problems.

It has become very apparent that my usual wit and repartee are significantly underrepresented today. So will just get out of the way and hope for a better day tomorrow. Till then.

12/04/2000

## don belk young

**From:** "don belk young" <donbelk@bellsouth.net>
**To:** "john downey" <jjones2742@aol.com>
**Sent:** Tuesday, December 05, 2000 5:56 PM
**Subject:** OK – ONE MORE TIME

Eydie, got your email. Thanks. I always assumed that you got to wait just as long in Arkansas or anywhere else as you do here. So it is reassuring to find that the efficiency rating of M.D.'s does exceed the normal variation. Got to have that comfort feeling that most people are normal. We have been tested a few times.

About keyboard skills. They can be acquired. All one needs is something commonly known as determination and basic hand/eye skills. Well, guess that lets John out on at least two counts. But he seems to be reasonably decent otherwise.

In the Birmingham News today was a brief item about the Methodist Church at five points south. Something about being back to business as usual after a fire of some kind a few weeks back. Assume John knows about it but just passing on info. Do you have the newspaper sent to Arkansas so you can keep up with what is happening around here? If we can make some arrangements, let us know. Also, if you would like for us to go by and look in the windows or something, just say so. We may do it anyhow under the pretension that we are being dutiful to our friends regardless of our motives. I don't think that we have any of those, anyhow. Especially the ulterior ones. I hear that they are very bad for both the ulterioree and the ulteriorer. Thought I was not going to find any nonsense there for awhile.

Talk about civic duty, conflicts of interest, etc. As you know, UAB plays basketball at Bradley U. in Peoria tonight. Peoria is in Illinois, about forty five miles from someplace in Iowa, but they hardly ever talk about that up there. I have relatives there so know all about it even though we never hear from them except for Xmas cards and class reunions.

In the meantime, the Board of the homeowners association scheduled a meeting to negotiate a three year contract for yard maintenance. Just found out that the Board meeting has two of the competing contractors coming to present detail info, so will need to disappear if I want to enjoy Gary Sanders et. al. Did you notice that Judge Sauls pronounces college as "electorial" and says Al instead of all?

If you need to know what the point of that last question, please hesitate to ask because it may take awhile to remember what the point of that last question is.

Woowoo has been to see three or four doctors today for routine stuff including a mammogram. Tells me that if I ever had one would never think of it as being anything but torture. But she has dutifully called—we have a rule that I must know where she is at all times except when I do not know.

The Bush/Gore or Gore/Bush, take your pick, soap opera picks up again and has not scheduled its last appearance. Talk about excitement. A real cliffhanger. My honest opinion is that Mr. Gore is the one hanging on the cliff by one fingernail, or maybe Tipper has put a suction kiss an him somewhere. He had better wish that..........another fill in the blank. I have no idea what they are trying to do now. Am just thankful that we do not any lawyers who want to explain it.

'Til the morrow.

12/05/2000

**don belk young**

---

**From:** "don belk young" <donbelk@bellsouth.net>
**To:** "john downey" <jjones2742@aol.com>
**Sent:** Wednesday, December 06, 2000 5:34 PM
**Subject:** THE MORROW


John, you do not need to use up any little gray cells regarding the question about why a coach pushes a player into a game that the player was already hurrying to get into. And here is the reason why. No one knows and never will. Would it not be comforting if all things human were so easy to understand.

Have you noticed any errors in any of these communications. First, of course, you must define what is an error. That is left to the reader. Because if a reader does not how to spell anything, that reader would not know whether any spelling errors had occurred. Any under those circumstances, which, unfortunately, are quite common, there would be fewer errors than have occurred when read by those of us who are fortunate to be more erudite and loquacious, especially when sentences are allowed to run on without any real meaning or substance and will contain so many spelling errors that it becomes impossible to continue without your head hurting, not to mention what hapens.to your hands and feet where the fingernails and toenails keep growing no matter what. Makes me tired and bored just to think about it and if you were writing this stuff as original copy without being too able to backspace or delete anything your bristles would start showing.

I believe that you admitted one time that you were a scholar. Perhaps it was some mumbling about what you would be if you could be whatever you wanted, or may have been a comment about what your mother thought you were or should have been. In a future issue—these promises are called teasers in the media—will bring to your attention observations of Alexander Tyler about the Athenian Republic which I suppose happened during the Athenian era. Probably has some Greek background, like feta cheese or black olives. And will certainly give it a shot.

We now proceed to the real reason for this memo and since I have forgotten what it was, that's it.

12/06/2000

**don belk young**

**From:** "don belk young" <donbelk@bellsouth.net>
**To:** "john downey" <jjones2742@aol.com>
**Sent:** Thursday, December 07, 2000 1:47 PM
**Subject:** WELL, THIS ONE IS DIFFERENT

Woowoo laughed so much reading some of the nonsense series that she sprained her chest. And that takes some doing, let me tell you.

Seriously, about midnight she was having chest pains and a "flushed" feeling, seemed to be near fainting, and was on the verge of panic when she woke me and immediately, I called 911. They arrived in about two minutes, six guys, two fire trucks, and one ambulance. She was feeling better but went to Brookwood and did a series of additional tests. A very nice young female doctor seemed to know what she was doing, called a cardiologist who said that Woowoo should be admitted to the hospital. So I came home about 4 a.m. Developments so far today are not conclusive at this time—more tests scheduled "sometime" and "may" be able to come home today. Update later.

Back to the fray. How are things in your home state by now. Do they have both sides of Main Street in Fort Smith blacktopped? And what about Hayti? Who would ever think that there is a place named Hayti near the bootheel of Missouri, but there it is, And a great place about 15 feet off the road to get roast beef and mashed potatoes and gravy. Wonder why these reminiscences come to mind. Tell you what, I have never got a handle on what the hell I am thinking about. Zooms all over the place and I just can't keep up. Like Socrates said, I reached out to get and it wasn't even there.

Did you notice the names of the bunch of females that were in attendance at Villa Rosa the other day. One of them was Judy and she does have a last name—Allison. Don't think she has ever driven a race car but she does know how to run around. Great personality. Reminds me of someone that we know very well. Has good presence, good sense of humor, and pathos and stuff like that. Has a tendency to iterate—that means doing things over and over—and has a good time doing it. Has such a good time that one has a tendency to think that it is as amusing as it was the first time. It is a quality to strive for and I hope that you get your share if you have missed any of it. For example, I suggested that she did not know a pissant from a toadfrog. She responded with a smile with a wry comment that it probably did not make a nickel's worth of difference.

For this installment, will use my file of inconsequential trivia to try to create the proper sense of balance between purpose and, I suppose, non-purpose because, once again, at the risk of creating another of those famous run-on sentences, it seemed like the thing to do at the time and, as Voltaire, or was It Volker—always got those two mixed up—once said to see Dick and Scotty about that. That occurred because Joe, as he came to be known, was a visionary and those visionaries have a hard time nailing down those loose thoughts running around. Maybe I are one, come to think about it. So remember to remind me that I am leaving. And "What bothers me most is that it doesn't bother you." Finally, when decanting wine, make sure that you tilt the paper cup and pour slowly to not 'bruise' the fruit of the vine.

As they say somewhere

Ciao.

12/07/2000

**don belk young**
_____

| | |
|---|---|
| **From:** | "don belk young" <donbelk@bellsouth.net> |
| **To:** | "john downey" <jjones2742@aol.com> |
| **Sent:** | Friday, December 08, 2000 12:56 PM |
| **Subject:** | TODAY IS THE DAY |

This may be the day of days. And then again it may not. See, there you go again.

Woowoo is home from Brookwood with another medication. This is one for antacid. Apparently that was the problem—reflux. That must be something that happens when your stomach does not know what else to with it. Wander how it got a name like that. Is that the same thing that radiators on cars used to do when they got too hot? Probably will never know We were going to ask Dr. Jones, yep, that was his name, but we thought he might tell us if we pressed it so let it go. So if you, Dr. Jones, know what the answer is, we do not want to know from you, either. Unless you can make it sound good.

UAB game tonight vs. Murray State. In my opinion, UAB needs to win this one. Mostly because that is better than losing and it looks good in the paper. Also makes those who are for UAB feel good and thus prevents wars and riots from breaking out. We sure do not want that, do we?

We are getting ready to go to a place called Meadowcraft. If I remember what we went for, will include that in a future report.

Also, in about twenty minutes, Florida is going to elect George W. Bush as President of the U.S. for four years beginning Jan. 20, 2001. Then we can all get back to work so we can pay taxes and stuff.

Hope you all are progressing OK.

12/09/2000

**don belk young**

| | |
|---|---|
| From: | "don belk young" <donbelk@bellsouth.net> |
| To: | "john downey" <jjones2742@aol.com> |
| Sent: | Friday, December 08,2000 4:27 PM |
| Subject: | A LITTLE MORE |

We finished but we didn't get done. That will also be the subject of a future note, maybe. The trip to Meadowcraft was a very pleasant drive, well it wasn't a drive through the mountains, but the sun was shining and we only had a couple of drivers who tried to compete by running us off the road. I have noticed that there is less of that than there was last week. But I think the long term trend is toward more or less letting all the drivers on the road, especially Interstate highways, do whatever they want to.

Talk about a full plate. You should see the calendar for December 18, 2000. Retirement for Ken Adams at 2:30, UFCU annual Board meeting and party at The Club at 4, Xmas party at Lovoy's from 4 'til whenever, and, most important of all, Woowoo has a birthday all day that day. She will be xxxxxxx, and x = 10.1428571428. And that is finite. As you can see, this is not nearly as complicated as Pi.

Reminds me that a cherry pie is waiting to be made so will get to it soon.

About Tallahassee. Some of it has to do with relatives living in Alabama. When this can be related to something else, will see whether it is still a capital idea. In the meantime, just do the best that you can and remember "Dirt and grease under the fingernails is a social no-no, as they tend to detract from a woman's jewelry and alter the taste of finger foods."

As they say in Guam "Alohaiaiah"

12/09/2000

## don belk young

| | |
|---|---|
| **From:** | "don belk young" <donbelk@bellsouth.net> |
| **To:** | "john downey" <jjones2742@aol.com> |
| **Sent:** | Saturday, December 09, 2000 12:35 PM |
| **Subject:** | ETC |

Update on Woowoo. After two days and many tests and a lot of inattention, Dr. Jones, yep, that was his name, concluded that must have been an attack or whatever you call it, of reflux. Seems that these symptoms—chest pain, shortness of breath, ulcers—can be identified with a lot of things including heart attack, emphysema, etc. And by process of elimination, blood tests, stress tests on the treadmill, x-rays, and monitoring are able to determine the most likely cause of such symptoms. So we now have a prescription for medication to help out.

Wish you had not asked about UAB basketball. You had my report about the Bradley defeat, away. Yeah, really away, up yonder around Iowa some-where. Then last night had a humiliating experience, managing to lose to Murray State in overtime 84-72. UAB had been 14 points ahead with about ten minutes to go, had been in the lead the entire game until it was tied in the last minute. Then were outscored 18-6 in overtime. Not a lot of fun in the G&G afterward.

Saw Mayor McCallum, He was telling Senator Rogers that he got to the game late because he had been out picking up leaves for his constituency. Thought it was a joke until I remembered that he is a detail, hands-on type of manager.

Need a little inspiration. One of the lesser philosophers opined that accom-plishment is 10% inspiration, 45% perspiration, and 72.6% desperation. Now I know that adds up to more than 127%, don't bother with the math, but wanted to demonstrate that there is more than one way of accomplishing. So will take the easy way and turn it all loose. Let's see what happens.

Davy Barry has been in touch again. He was not very subtle about it, but let it be known that it was highly unlikely that anything that has been written herewould qualify as any kind of journalism so he sees no need to do anything unless it is outside his range, which is 48.5 miles from Miami. That is the point where you disappear into the Everglades forever and no one ever knows whether you lived happily ever alter or not. The best guess is that the mango trees and manatees are not to be sneezed at. There must be the makings of a limerick in there somewhere. The limerick will have to come later. For now, here is one that you probably have not heard for two or three months. "The sex of a bee is hard to see, but he can tell and so can she, and that is why in times like these, there are so many sons of bees."

As they say in the Everglades,

YUK.

12/09/2000

## don belk young

| | |
|---|---|
| **From:** | "don belk young" <donbelk@bellsouth.net> |
| **To:** | "john downey" <jjones2742@aol.com> |
| **Sent:** | Saturday, December 09, 2000 12:54 PM |
| **Subject:** | ETC. |

Wish you had not asked. About UAB basketball, that is. Lost to Bradley at Peoria. Think I sent that info. And last night, well, I do not want to talk about it. After being ahead by sixteen points with about ten minutes to go in the second half, managed to let Murray State tie the game with a three pointer. Then did not do anything in overtime and got beat up pretty bad, losing 84-72. 1 think Murray State is located somewhere, but do not know and do not care. I think that qualifies as ignorant or apathetic, or both. But I have always wanted to be just like you and maybe am now qualified.

Update on Woowoo. Apparently reflux can cause symptoms that relate to chest pain, emphysema, ulcers, shortness of breath—is that the same as emphysema—and requires many tests and quite a bit of time to establish. After two days Dr. Jones, yep, that is his name, said that seems to be the basic problem. So we have a prescription that will help out, we hope.

Need some inspiration about now. Do not seem to have any and can't find any perspiration either. One of the lesser philosophers, during his politalk period, or it may have been Chaucer, said that accomplishment was 10% perspiration and 50% inspiration and approximately 72% desperation. Have you ever noticed how approximations tend to be more exact than non-approximations. Yes, I know that those numbers add up to more than approximately 132% but we have recently recanted and are thinking about becoming surreptitious do-gooders. I told you that Dave Barry had tried to ridicule my infringement on his type of irresponsible journalism, but have learned that he has determined without a shred of doubt that he has no competition within 48.5 miles of Miami. That is the point where you disappear into the Everglades and find solace among the mango trees and manatees. Might be able to use that alliteration in a limerick. Along the lines of mango trees and manatees make me sneeze and wheeze and think of bees. This does not qualify as a limerick but you probably have not heard it for three or four months. So "The sex of a bee is hard to see, but he can tell and so can she, and that is why in times like these, there are so many sons of bees."

This is really embarrassing. Well, not really because there is only one way that I can be embarrassed and it has already been tried and failed. But the point is, must be one here somewhere. I thought that this version of today's missile had been lost when the machine experienced some trauma, but it was hiding where things go when you get interrupted. So I tried to duplicate what had been done. So will just send both of them even there is some duplication because of my ability to recreate that which has already been created. Unusual talent there but needs some refinement, especially in the modesty mode.

And so we go forward in all directions.

12/09/2000

## don belk young

| | |
|---|---|
| **From:** | "don belk young" <donbelk@bellsouth.net> |
| **To:** | "john downey" <jjones2742@aol.com> |
| **Sent:** | Sunday, December 10, 2000 10:59 AM |
| **Subject:** | GERD |

**Has it ever to you occurred, that you could learn a new word**

**Unless you are a real live nerd, and your gray cells had been stirred**

**If you were a horse and got spurred, or an alley cat and got defurred**

**You would think of an explanatory and probably descriptive new word**

**To describe your situation which would have to be called absurd**

**So when reflux knocks, and you go to that place with the docs,**

**Your imagination gets stirred, your vision is not blurred,**

**And you really do learn a new word. It is called GERD!!!**

You do not need to keep this one for posterity. But I am not making this up, GERD is now a part of our vocabulary. It is an acronym for gastroesophageal reflux disease, commonly referred to as reflux.

But on to more serious stuff. You may have noticed that my typing speed is so spectacular that a shortcut occurs every once in awhile by skipping over a word. It is a clever way of saving space (got to save the trees, you know) and not using so much paper. And inspires the reader to think. Do you not get a thrill when you try to read something that makes no because a key has been out. If you can complete that sentence without having a stroke, it means at least two things. Your arteries to your head are oxygenizing the gray cells and filling in the blanks—in the sentence, not in the brain, and the other thing is, uh, oh, oh, we may be on the brink of something and it does not bode well. Oh well, we did not want to be boded anyhow. The final test of your cognitive (that is the same thing as being able to add two and two) powers is to be able to tell with an exact count how many words have been omitted in the first two and the last three messages. There was 11.5 left out of those in the middle so you do not need to think about that at all.

Speaking of counting, here's one from Florida. "If you don't like the way we count in Florida, take I95 to one of the other 56 states!"

*Th th th that's it.*

12/10/2000

## don belk young

**From:**         "don belk young" <donbelk@bellsouth.net>
**To:**           "john downey" <jjones2742@aol.com>
**Sent:**         Monday, December 11,2000 9:56 AM
**Subject:**      ELECTION DAY MAYBE

We are waiting with baited breath for the results of the Supreme Court. My breath is baited with scotch and is unbearable. Even I can hardly stand it. The waiting, I mean. We have just about decided to let Bush have it as far as we are concerned. He seems to be working harder on his ranch than Al Gore is at the Naval Observatory. Wonder if he has ever observed anything from there, like dimples on the moon or something erotic like that.

Today is not just another day no matter how you look at it. We looked at it very carefully and sent Yumyum out to look at it from under the deck at the back of the house. Then I looked at it when I went to the mailbox (thought about you, John, bet you miss going to the mailbox) and noticed that it was different than yesterday, and by all appearances was different than it is going to be tomorrow. I can say that with a great deal of confidence since tomorrow never gets here. As you know from previous notes, I am a scholar about philosophers from Descartes to Sam Donaldson and not much escapes my attention. Every one of the scholars that I have the privilege of never knowing, with one exception of a fellow who said his name was John Jones, has said that "everything will be Ok tomorrow." Why don't we just leave it at that since this is obviously not going anywhere.

Have several errands to do today. I have found that retirement provides one with the opportunity to do errands the way they were intended to be done. The most effective way is to just forget about. Doesn't make any difference whether you forget about it intentionally or just plain forget. Either way they frequently go away and place themselves in the category of things that did not deserve to be done anyhow. Then there are those that really, really need to happen, like buying bananas or sharpening the razor strop. You probably think that should be strap. Look it up.

All other errands are caught up in that great middle section where they may or may not get any attention unless you are what is called retired and have enough time to give it a try. One of the dangers here is that the more things you try to do the more opportunity you have to get it wrong. Odds are about 2-1, one way or the other. And what bothers me most is that it doesn't bother you. So I suggest that you start hanging around with a better class of losers.

About Tallahassee. One of the intriguing things is how it came to be spelled with one t, two h's and s's and l's but has three asses, I mean a's. And more about that may or may not be part of the final dissertation on the capitalization of Florida. They sold junk bonds, I think. Wish those little gray cells would hold still long enough to make some sense out of at some of this.

From the treetop in Honolulu—Aloha!!!!!
grandon and woowoo
everyone is ENTITLED to a struggle

12/11/2000

**don belk young**

---

| | |
|---|---|
| **From:** | "don belk young" <donbelk@bellsouth.net> |
| **To:** | "john downey" <jjones2742@aol.com> |
| **Sent:** | Tuesday, December 12, 2000 1:31 PM |
| **Subject:** | AND ON WE GO |

QUODLIBET. Now there is a word for you. And discovered at a most appropriate time since we have had several discussions involving philosophy and philosophers, all the way from Demosthenes, who couldn't talk without a mouthful of rocks, to John Downey Jones, who can talk without saying anything. But enough of the routine insults and on to your edification. Quodlibet is a theological discussion point—a theological question put forth as an exercise for discussion. I think Frank, my brother, and I had these discussions as often as once a day back around the summer of 1930. These discussions usually had a special tone about them and did not require any vocabulary skills. He would say "Yes, it is." and I would say "No, it ain't." On alternate days we would reverse the dialogue. We thought we were having an imbroglio, a complicated situation, a confusing, messy situation, especially one that involves disagreement or intrigue, until our Mom would grab both of us by both arms—never could figure out how she was able to do that except she had been a school teacher—and tell us to shut up.

Great things continue to be part of our everyday life. Had an epiphany yesterday but I couldn't reach it so it became swollen and itchy and then went away as quickly as it had occurred. So my question to you is: Can you have an epiphany and not even know it, or do they always leave you with a droll sense of humor.

Also yesterday we triumphed over another potential adversity by hanging a Christmas wreath outside the front door of our modest home. Other than a brilliant outburst involving use of last year's lights for an extension cord, it was not really that much of a big deal. For instance, the 97 cent extension cord that I had so carefully selected became just another miscellaneous item hanging in the garage. And it was necessary to buy a box of nails for $2.37, approx. .0237 cents each. So the total out-of-pocket expense of the wreath installation was less than 3 cents, not counting overhead. The good news is that it looks great.

Something to ponder. if you have never heard of a feature involving automobiles called "freewheeling in," you will have to read my explanation if I can think of one.

So until freewheeling in or some equally absurd topic, remember the Maine, the Alamo and 10 cent beer.

grandon and woowoo
everyone is ENTITLED to a struggle

12/12/2000

## don belk young

| | |
|---|---|
| **From:** | "don belk young" <donbelk@bellsouth.net> |
| **To:** | "john downey" <jjones2742@aol.com> |
| **Sent:** | Wednesday, December 13, 2000 11:23 AM |
| **Subject:** | ET. AL. |

Thanks for asking. Woowoo is getting along OK. Think her medicine may need to be changed and is trying to talk to Dr. Jordan about that. I guess the good news is that reflux is better than a heart attack or advanced emphysema.

Made a note of Eydie's phone number in room 780 and Woowoo will be calling. I hope that these notes provide you-all with a little comic relief. But I had some once and couldn't tell whether it was because of something I ate or not. As another of those great philosophers, Diogenes, said "If you have someone eating out of your hand, you had better count your fingers."

UAB basketball tonight here in Bartow Arena. Chattanooga. UAB should win easily, but that was the situation with Murray State, also. Eric Batchelor was quoted in the morning paper as ready "to step up and be a leader." That's OK with me but would rather he just win the game. Maybe that's the same thing. After tonight do not have another home game until Virginia Commonwealth on Dec. 30. The team will be in California and Hawaii during the holidays. I have not been invited.

Too cold to play golf today so will have to be satisfied with a meeting about the Credit Union budget for next year. It has the potential of being about a 1/2 on a scale of 1 to 10.

A couple of quotations from my file of inconsequential trivia.

"Endowed professors are like diamonds. They last forever, seldom appear in public, and don't come cheap."

"Virtue is its own punishment." This one requires deep thinking.

"Blessed are those who arrange diverse elements into masterful works of fiction for they shall be called Dean of Students."

"If a statement begins with 'as a matter of fact` whatever follows is likely to be a downright lie."

As they say in Timbuktu "Me and Tim a fishin' went, etc."
grandon and woowoo
everyone is ENTITLED to a struggle

12/13/2000

## don belk young

| | |
|---|---|
| **From:** | "don belk young" <donbelk@bellsouth.net> |
| **To:** | "john downey" <jjones2742@aol.com> |
| **Sent:** | Thursday, December 14, 2003 2:37 PM |
| **Subject:** | Re: ET. AL. AND A LITTLE MORE |

John, there was no attachment to the Dec 14 epistle so do not know what the complication might be. Hope you can open it since these are getting better all the time and this was a good one. You surely are aware by now that it required a certain level of erudition to know what these soliloquies really mean. But in case it has escaped you, they do not mean a damn thing. Just filler material to keep the blank and empty spaces in the cranium from becoming predominant, if you get the drift. What it is is exercising the little gray cells, otherwise atrophy and misdemeanors may occur.

Yes, we are also glad that the election is now over. We had anticipated possibly having a rollicking good crisis that we could see firsthand, like an asteroid hurtling toward earth or Al Gore sidling up to a karaoke machine. Something. Anything. UAB tried to have a crisis last night, very much like the one when they played Murray State. But they dodged it and managed to win 65-59 without overtime. I did observe that it took 20 minutes to play the last 1 min, 37 sec. Most unusual. Let me know if you want more details and will try to make up something.

Also in the news today. UAB will try to sell, at auction, the 57 acre lakeside retreat at Chelsea on Dec. 21. I think it has been idle for a long, long time. Was one of those Hospital projects that just did not work. I would ask Jim Moon about it, but he gives shorter non-answers than I do so probably would not learn anything.

A previous note referred to Alexander Tyler who wrote about why voting should be restricted. He was not writing about the United States. Over a hundred years ago he was writing about the fall of the Athenian Republic. "A democracy cannot exist as a permanent form of government. It can only exist until the voters discover that they can vote themselves money from the public treasure. From that moment on the majority always votes for the candidates promising the most money from the public treasury, with the result that a democracy always collapses over loose fiscal policy followed by a dictatorship. The average age of the world's great civilizations has been two hundred years. These nations have progressed through the following sequence: from bondage to spiritual faith, from spiritual faith to great courage, from courage to liberty, from liberty to abundance, from abundance to selfishness, from selfishness to complacency, from complacency to apathy, from apathy to dependence, from dependency back to bondage." Please excuse this departure from the silliness theme that has dominated these notes, but ran across this and, after thinking about it, I think the U.S. is in the abundance to selfishness stage, so may not be around for the next round of bondage.

Fellow says he knew he was going to live to a hundred because he was 50 and was half dead.

Scotty was at the UAB game last night with Alice, Kitty and Jane. I asked Jane for Paul Braun's address, which is 1802 Frank Hall Circle, Jonesboro, Arkansas 72401 – ph. 870-802-4917.

From Alabama – you all come back, ya heah.

12/14/2000

## don belk young

**From:** "don belk young" <donbelk@bellsouth.net>
**To:** "john downey" <jjones2742@aol.com>
**Sent:.** Friday, December 15, 2000 10:21 AM
**Subject:** FRIDAY

If you don't care where you are, you ain't lost. Dionysus said that just before he lost his marbles. But he had those marbles that get lost easily because they are round and can roll into corners and other dark places. These almost always are found by getting stepped on. I must have been a marble in a previous life. Or maybe it was because I was a wee lad. Got stepped on by a horse once when I was barefooted. Remind me to relate that experience. It has something to with digging a well. I was supposedly in charge of the horse but she did not know that. It really is an intriguing story and can be made into a tale that would be unbelievable with a little imagination. And my imagination is very little most of the time.

But I have a lemma for you. Just when you had become accustomed to epiphanous happenings, here comes a lemma. To save you the trouble of thinking up some meaning for the word lemma, here it is. It is a proposition that is assumed to be true in order to test the validity of another proposition. So the next time you get a proposition, ask the propositioner if he or she is using the lemma technique. Talk about erudite!!! So the lemma is – "there is nothing so small that it can't be blown out of proportion." Now to test this proposition let us assume that we do not care where we are. Does this point to a conclusion that if you do not care where you are, you ain't lost. Or have we already dealt with that. As you can see, this is apparently a day of density. Density used intentionally here. The reason is elusive but must have something to do with gloom, despair and agony as they used to say on Heehaw. As a sophisticated person you may have never heard of "Heehaw." Will expand on it only if requested in writing. After all, it should be evident by now that I do not waste my time babbling about inconsequential trivia any more than is necessary to just barely get by.

Every great writer can attribute success to a confidant who can offer constructive criticism and I am blessed in that respect. I get blessed (special meaning there) each time a word is misspelled or omitted and thus have heightened awareness about maintaining standards of excellence. I mention this only to assure you that it is not necessary for you to point out mistakes. I would be embarrassed for you and would most likely—100% probability—ignore you, anyhow. If it became so critical that it could be classified as a crisis, I would remind you that a crisis is when you can't say "Let's forget the whole thing." Getting convoluted again. May be recovering, but have a sense that it is about time to declare intellectual bankruptcy. And on that upbeat note,

As the Rottweiler said to the Dachshund, go find your own tail
grandon and woowoo
everyone is ENTITLED to a struggle

12/15/2000

## don belk young

**From:** "don belk young" <donbelk@bellsouth.net>
**To:** "john downey" <jjones2742@aol.com>
Sent Saturday, December 16, 2000 12:04 PM
**Subject:** AND NOW

*Today we will write in Italian. I assume that is the origin of italics. As history will tell you if you will only listen, the Italians, who were known as Romans once upon a time, will tell you anything to get what they want, and they have more Italian babies than any other nation. Also, they were so good at writing history that their system of worldwide domination lasted almost 500 years. I have always thought that they would have been better off to let someone else get the credit but you know how they are. 91.36% of them do not even know the difference between bologna and lumbago, except that they end in a vowel so must be some kind of pasta.*

*Got the "recently acquired humor" email from Bob Glaze. The one about lunch will begin at 12:15, correction 12:00 reminded me of those lunches that you enjoyed so much that you cancelled all of your afternoon appointments. Of course, you had already missed the 1:30 and 2:30 meetings.*

*UAB is at Fresno State tonight. The sports item today has already reported the score—65-59. I was good at predictions once but got over it during a bout of antipasto—that's another of those pasta creations.*

-----------------------------------------------------------------------

*It is quite apparent that I am lost. The sense of timing so critical to the creative output is also lost so will give up for now. Besides, it's time to run the vacuum and put together a cherry pie.*

*Until another time, hasta la vista and lotsa bologna,*

grandon and woowoo
everyone is ENTITLED to a struggle

12/16/2000

## don belk young

| | |
|---|---|
| **From:** | "don belk young" <donbelk@bellsouth.net> |
| **To:** | "john downey" <jjones2742@aol.com> |
| **Sent:** | Sunday, December 17, 2000 3:43 PM |
| **Subject:** | OOPS |

Just now found out that the draft that I was working on yesterday some-how got sent on its way. Surely you can tell that these carefully thought out and cleverly worded epistles do not get to go out of here with a lot of careless scrutiny. On to current events.

UAB managed to lose by 20 points at Fresno State last night.

Did you get your share of rodomontade after finding that it was not a con-trolled substance. You may have found out that if you already have the maximum amount allowed, as Luke said, that's all there is. In my opinion you have all you need and, since it is not my purpose to make decisions about the stuff, you may have all you will ever get. The good news is that once you have it, no matter how much you use your cup remaineth full. A most extraordinary thing, indeed. You may not be able to do the research necessary to get the full and accurate meaning from any other source so will share it with you right now. Rodomontade is a pretentious, self-im-portant, or self-indulgent boasting, speech, or behavior. Thought you might want to know so that when you are confronted by someone that you do not like, actually have no use for whatsoever and they accuse you of rodomontading (that's 3rd person present singular usage), you can just say that you already knew that and was about to tell him or her the same thing.

You will recall the famous picture of Adlai Stevenson's shoe that needed repair. It is a shame that this image has caused almost everyone except a few scholars to forget the soliloquy that he spoke—"Man does not live by words alone despite the fact that sometimes he has to eat them." In closing today, I would ask just one thing. Please do ask me to eat my words. I am sure that several that have been seen here in the last few days would be hard to swallow and something like rodomontade or cellulite could lead to severe indigestion, perhaps reflux. And having already experienced reflux second hand, so to speak, I already know that I do not want any of that.

But, as Cleopatra told Caesar, I am not prone to argue.
grandon and woowoo
everyone is ENTITLED to a struggle

12/17/2000

## don belk young

| | |
|---|---|
| **From:** | "don belk young" <donbelk@bellsouth.net> |
| **To:** | "john downey" <jjones2742@aol.com> |
| **Sent:** | Monday, December 18, 2000 12:46 PM |
| **Subject:** | GOT IT |

Your birthday card was a winner. We enjoyed seeing it and watching it, and printed a copy. Thanks. Thanks. Woowoo is now 70 something and you had better not make anything out of that that is not intended. If you do now know what is intended, it is probably best to not guess. It is not recorded in historical annals but the last time someone attempted to guess what woowoo intended was the recipient of just exactly what she intended for them to get. Just let it go at that.

About ready to start on our multiple adventures for today. May send postscript around midnight if we survive the annual party at Lovoy's. But then again may not. You know how it is. Can you imagine any more bankrupt brain than one that can use a lot of words without saying anything. It's a gift.

As my Dad would say, come back when you have something to say.
grandon and woowoo
everyone is ENTITLED to a struggle

12/19/2000

**don belk young**

| | |
|---|---|
| **From:** | "don belk young" <donbelk@bellsouth.net> |
| **To:** | "john downey" <jjones2742@aol.com> |
| **Sent:** | Tuesday, December 19, 2000 9:53 AM |
| **Subject:** | SNOW KIDDING |

Do you know what swans eat? It is not a matter of extreme urgency but any insight you have toward a solution of this question would be better than anything we have wondered about lately. You see, during the snow-storm this morning, which must have gone on for at least 17 minutes, we became concerned about the comfort zone of our friends, the swans. Not the football player family, we are talking about real swans here. We both remembered that mairzy doats and dozy doats and little lamzy divy, but could not find a swan in there anywhere. Yumyum went out during the snowstorm to be sure that the protective moat did not float away so we have survived nicely. But the day is shaping up as one of those in which the highlight will be a trip to Food World for cat food. Would get some swan food but unless you can help right away on this burning issue we may just have to let it burn until it goes out.

Have you thought anymore about any possible explanation of anything. And more specifically, what in the world would cause any sensible adult to indulge in a stream of consciousness style of writing when with a little less effort that same person could do nothing. You may read into this an admission that this note and my truck are in the same situation. Neither one of them is going anywhere. And the sooner they get there the better.

Crumhorn is the word of the day and it has not yet been defined by the Incas or the Phoenicians so will remain obscure as far as we are concerned. That is the final word on that.

You know about soliloquies so surely it is not necessary to explain. It may seem repetitive to iterate over again. Like those well-known deja vus but our yesterday went like this: we were struck with pellucidity. This is a lot different than snowflakes or any other kind of flakes. It has nothing to do with any flakes of any kind. It is simply a state of consciousness when everything is "easy to understand or clear in meaning." You can understand how exciting this is because it had never happened before. You may have noticed, for instance, how unclear all of the above seems to be. So if you can obtain even a small amount of pellucidity (adv.) you will be much better informed and I, for one, wish for you all you can get.

As the mule said when he was asked whether he would like some mairzy doats, he lifted his tail and said "aphoo."

No promises, but maybe it will get better by tomorrow.
grandon and woowoo
everyone is ENTITLED to a struggle

12/19/2000

**don belk young**

| | |
|---|---|
| **From:** | "don belk young" <donbelk@bellsouth.net> |
| **To:** | "john downey" <jjones2742@aol.com> |
| **Sent:** | Wednesday, December 20, 2000 11:19 AM |
| **Subject:** | ESSAY DU JOUR |

As I recall a du jour is something like a fon du lac. Then again that may be someplace in Wisconsin or some other foreign country. Both of my friends suggested that I would be hoisted by my own petard but I had a retarded petard and it was so small that it never did work. Probably better to have a retarded petard than a pedantic petard. The pedantic one would be unbending, mentally speaking, and could leave one with a retarded brain from indulging in thoughtful discussions that used up any reserves of little cells.

This was a happening many years ago when I couldn't even spell petard so had not mentioned it until now when the spelling came to me in a blinding, spasmodic, yes, it was another epiphany. And to this day there is no petard that is more unhallowed.

We can now proceed to the thought of the day but can't seem to find it. If you happen to be there when it comes by, please send it along. Meantime, the news of the day is that we are finally having a winter. The doomsayers have started complaining about global freezing. Civilization is thought to exist only within about 400 million meters of the equator. Seems a shame to waste all those condominiums in Orange Beach. The good news is that this is not likely to occur for at least 30 years.

A related problem is the likelihood of being afflicted with irreversible, irreverent irredentism. Perhaps I can simplify for you. I know that you have limited access to new ideas and day to day revelations, so just remember that it is not necessary to know what you are talking about to convince anyone listening to you that you do not know what you are talking about. Just move your lips.

Would send along the bad news but there was not any today. The radio is silent, the TV is black, the newspaper is a blank, so everything must be OK for now. And on that note of serenity, peacefulness, and tranquility, we will just get out of the way.

Grandon and woowoo
everyone is ENTITLED to a struggle

12/20/2000

## don belk young

**From:**   "don belk young" <donbelk@bellsouth.net>
**To:**     "john downey" <jjones2742@aol.com>
**Sent:**   Thursday, December 21, 2000 10:36 AM
**Subject:** ARKANSAS

Overheard in a quaint town in Western Arkansas. "Where's this road go to?" the traveler asked. "I've been livin' here fer years, 'n' I ain't seen it go no place." It seems incredible that this exchange between de Soto, who discovered Arkansas, and the local Indian chief, would have been recorded for history. It occurred in 1541 or 1542 and probably contributed to the myth that de Soto was lost and had no idea what he was trying to do. Later on Orval Faubus came along and steered the state in the wrong direction one more time. Then Winthrop Rockefeller came along and did a couple of things and not much happened until this used car salesman named Jones came along and they lived happily ever after.

When I failed the entrance exam to the school of erudidity, applied for a learner's permit to be a raconteur. Failed to get any negative references— one or two would have been adequate—so got left out of that also. May take a shot at recidivism one more time.

UAB basketball is in Hawaii. First of three games in three days starts this evening. Watson Brown is getting good press in his role as offensive coach for the Gray team in the Blue-Gray game in Montgomery. 32 degrees this a.m. Just right for the rain to freeze but seems to be a little warmer so may have dodged that problem. We may go to Trussville just for the heck of it. Will give me a chance to adapt to a style of driving a car that will take full advantage of tips that a very limited number (one) have had the opportunity to take advantage of. Our combined age is 147; average is 73 1/2, and that is the exact number of helpful suggestive and constructive criticisms that can be anticipated. The 1/2 can only be obtained by ignoring the other half of one of the suggestions. This is an unweighted system of averaging based on the volume and the tone and has nothing to do with the politics of personal destruction so often noticed in certain places that will go unmentioned, especially with the knowledge that these words may be brought to the attention of more than one critic.

We have a girl to attend to so must go.

Rather than make you wait until a later edition to enlighten about girl, it simply means a social obligation, like taking Woowoo to lunch at the Chocolate Soup somewhere in St. Clair County, or perhaps someplace else.

So for now it is just "Hacienda." That's Hawaiian for "where's your teepee."
grandon and woowoo
everyone is ENTITLED to a struggle

12/21/2000

**don belk young**

| | |
|---|---|
| **From:** | "don belk young" <donbelk@bellsouth.net> |
| **To:** | "john downey" <jjones2742@aol.com> |
| **Sent:** | Friday, December 22, 2000 5:52 FM |
| **Subject:** | PIGMY INDEED |

We are in complete agreement with your admission that reason no. 3 is applicable to your inability to receive these messages. But would argue with the premise that the pigmy principle is at work here. Probably more of an elf situation; robotic, mentally inferior, and of questionable stature in a non-physical sense. It is just beyond our capacity—as you can tell, our credentials in the erudite world are hardly worth mentioning, so we seldom or never make such claims—to grasp the significance of being pigmytized. Brings images of not being able to see and possibly losing your balance. You heard that old controller's never die, they just lose their balance. But wait!!! What you are is a member of the elves of erudition in the more optimistic meaning. And that is better, believe me, than being a gnome or a mote or a mite. Do not know what any of these things are but instinct tells me that neither you nor I want to be one.

Have you thought about Cyclops. Did he have one huge eye that was myopic or astigmatized or something that made it useless except when he went to tie his shoes and then he usually fell over and his eye fell out and he felt useless. Lot of feelings there. That's the American way, you know. How does it feel is the most common question heard from Oprah et al. And the most common answer is that the one being asked is a victim of something. Victimized, Pygmytized, Astigmatized. Who knows. The Shadow knows.

The Holidays approacheth. And I think I will also.

Hope you have a full recovery and are able to recoup your scruples in time to put them to the use for which they were intended. The warranty expires when you remove the tags from the mattress and once scruples are lost, they seldom return, so take advantage of this opportunity to start over and perhaps you will go all the way and become a giant of erudition.

We will be watching for the slightest evidence of sanity in both outgoing and incoming messages.

As the French pigmy said.... "oui." Wee, get it.
grandon and woowoo
everyone is ENTITLED to a struggle

12/22/2000

## don belk young

| | |
|---|---|
| From: | "don belk young" <donbelk@bellsouth.net> |
| To: | "john downey" <jjones2742@aol.com> |
| Sent: | Saturday, December 23, 2000 2:18 PM |
| Subject: | NO STATIONERY |

As a follow-up to your dilemma about opening email from here. An option in this system is to use "stationery." That may have been in use in a few notes, so have avoided that this time, I think. Let me know if this easier because, as the noted theorist theorized, nothing in the world is more dangerous than sincere ignorance or conscientious stupidity. And you can tell them that I said so.

Billy Brashier and I made 4 dozen walnut crescents this morning. We had an annual routine for many, many years of baking these delicacies, but for several years including his four years in the Navy we had "forgotten." When he suggested that we should reinstate the family tradition, I readily agreed, We were able to negotiate the use of a local kitchen, the one downstairs,and this morning at 8 a.m. proceeded to prepare the year 2000 run. Ask Woowoo if they are OK. Somehow they have been disappearing with great regularity.

Got your Xmas card in today's mail. Thanks for keeping us on your list. As you know, we are not your average suburban middle class retirees and often do things that we did not intend to and at other times we hardly ever do what someone (anyone) else thought would happen. Keeps you on your toes, and sometimes on your heels. Speaking of heels, remember this one "Time wounds all heels."

I wrote about something that we did one day last week. But I wrote about it before we did it and then it didn't happen, but have forgotten which event it was. So go back, if you are able to get your old mail, and pick out something that you thought was sort of dumb when it was mentioned and assume that it did not occur. If you decide, using this criteria, that everything mentioned would be better not happening, just eliminate the whole thing. But remember that I have written copies of each of these and a reserve copy in the wastebasket, so they will most likely be preserved in some form. We may go over towards Vincent after awhile. Will be on the lookout for a cave with walls that could be used to paint these messages on. In acrylic. In order to preserve the seminality of it all.

I'll bet that you never considered the possibility that a dissertation like this could be reduced so that it would fit on a pinhead.

Will explain that another time. Still owe you the Tallahassee saga. There was a duel involved.

As Teresa's mother, not Mother Teresa said, "Truth is the daughter of time." She was confused or they say in some circles, addled. She was so addled that she was trying to tell someone goodbye and was heard to say "Addleoo." No one explained. We will never know.

12/23/2000

**don belk young**

| | |
|---|---|
| **From:** | "don belk young" <donbelk@bellsouth.net> |
| **To:** | "john downey" <jjones2742@aol.com> |
| **Sent:** | Sunday, December 24, 2000 10:04 AM |
| **Subject:** | RESENT MAIL |

John, let me know if you received past issues that you can read. I copied them without the stationery heading switch turned on. If that works, you will be most fortunate to benefit from the hours and hours of work that has been put into the creation of these creations, and I would be remiss without giving credit to all of those who have of been helpful with constructive criticism and other nonsense about missing and misspelled words. That has already been explained with great care to as to render the creator blameless. So here are the decision rules.

No. 1. If you like it, it's mine.
No. 2 If you do not like it, it's not mine.

Forgot to finish what I started. You should have received a message each day starting with November 27. So if you do not have them, let me know what days are missing or could not be opened, and will resend. And will not be offended very much if you say that you wish that they would go away, and will continue anyhow. My publisher has suggested that it could be put into book form sort of like Sears Roebuck catalogues and used for the utilitarian purposes that last year's Sears catalog was used for before we had inside plumbing. This usage was the first known situation that could be defined as recycling and a plaque will soon be nailed to the outside wall of the Jonessonium Institute to commemorate this historical occasion.

UAB managed to lose two out of three in Hawaii. Looks more and more like a very long season and a very short post season.

The plan for this email was to be based on Plutarch and the wisdom that has benefited the world ever since he stopped mouthing off those Greek platitudes that even the Romans could not understand. Then it occurred to me that one could get labeled as a liberal and libeled all at the same time. I did not want to be any of these so have refrained from any use of anything wise. Also it is in keeping with previous messages that nonsense is the order of the day, and a side order of hash browns would go down better than "a one egg pudding." With apologies to Plutarch or whoever it was who said that, gotta go.

12/24/2000

## don belk young

| | |
|---|---|
| **From:** | "don belk young" <donbelk@bellsouth.net> |
| **To:** | "john downey" <jjones2742@aol.com> |
| **Sent:** | Monday, December 25, 2000 2:17 PM |
| **Subject:** | XMAS |

Happy Holiday to you-all. Your note said Eydie would have a pass and that Henry and Michael would be there, so we hope that you remembered how to do stuffed turkey or whatever you are supposed to do. And do it right. Here's how to do a turkey.

> Next Thanksgiving, next Thanksgiving,
> Save your bread, save your bread,
> Stuff it up your turkey, stuff it up your turkey,
> MAKE SURE HE'S DEAD.

Be sure to let me know if you were blessed with those emails that were sent again. The label on the first one did not mean that we resented sending them again. Just that it was again mailed, i.e. resent. Anyhow, if that system is working, will send others that you did not receive.

Now to the subject of the day. It is around here somewhere. Oh, before we do that. Heard from my private angel the other day. He also is chief of staff to Abraham Lincoln, and told me about a TO DO list that he and Abe are working on. 1. Free the slaves and unite the country. 2. Think of a fancy way to say 87 years ago. He had tried eight decades and seven years but didn't think it sounded quite right. 3. Beef up security at Ford's Theater.

Went to see Davis 'nem early today. Well, got there before 9 o'clock and had some special baked grits that Woowoo made; then got into the monkey bread. Yep, that is the name of the stuff. Let me know if you need any recipes. Michael is coming by this afternoon; have not heard from Cynthia about their plans (they are in Memphis). Will be at Geoffrey's tomorrow for Natalie's birthday (17).

Something just came over me. Feels like we are about to be serendipitous. Have been led to believe that serendipity is "a natural gift for making useful discoveries by accident." Well, we have had our share of accidents so there must be some serendipity in there somewhere.

Today is the first day of Christmas and is the beginning of that thing about the twelve days which end on Jan. 6. And guess what happens on Jan. 6 Never mind, I will just tell you. Jan. 6 is the day of Epiphany and that is what the twelfth day of Christmas is all about. If you think that this was a planned occurrence because of frequent reference to epiphany before, including having one or two, you may be right. But probably not.

You are already under a great deal of stress in anticipation of full, comprehensive explanation about putting memos on pinheads and how Tallahassee got to be where it is. Well, add this to your future edification—a special rendering of the twelve days of Xmas.

Got to get to work on that. Will put the gray matter to work. One final titillation, which you surely need. White matter is the same as gray matter except that it is myelinated. One more thing. Remind me to tell you about the location of the mistletoe. It can be discussed in hushed tones but cannot be talked about out loud or in mixed company unless the company was mixed before you got there. And even my talents cannot deal with writing any further about that or anything else, so will stop.

12/25/2000

## don belk young

**From:**   "don belk young" <donbelk@bellsouth.net>
**To:**     "john downey" <jjones2742@aol.com>
**Sent:**   Tuesday, December 26, 2000 10:23 AM
**Subject:** HUMBUG HAS HAD IT

Psephology. Phonetically speaking, psephology could pass for something that you need Depends for. But actually, and this is the truth as revealed in Hypocrisy, psephology is "the statistical study of elections." It was used by the Greeks—those guys and gals got into just about everything—when they used rocks to vote. Remember that. When you showed up at the agora, now known as a voting booth, you were handed a rock and would throw it at the one that you did not want to be elected. When the loser had been rocked to death and thrown over a cliff, the survivor was declared the winner. This worked fine until someone discovered democracy and we have had disputed elections up until recently when the Supreme Court of Florida ruled that all previous elections were invalid and declared William Howard Taft to be acting head honcho until further notice.

Other than Natalie's 17th birthday, and the twins Emily and Haley are 5, December 26 is commonly known as the day after Christmas. This may be the one that the British call Boxing Day. Lest you are so boorish as to think that the term Boxing Day has something to do with pugilism, permit to inform you that you are wrong again. You need to quit doing that until you learn to grovel gracefully. But we digress. Boxing Day means that you put that unwanted, recycled so-called gift of love, back into the Box and return it to whatever shop it was obtained from. That is the formal book definition. I have another way of expressing it, but Eydie might disapprove so will refrain for now. If you can't stand it and must know, we can discuss it some other time.

We will probably do something tomorrow that will provide me with some material to concoct another fable. I have done some research in connection with sartorius so you need not look it up. Will answer all your questions if you will list them in order of importance. Or even if you don't. This is just another service that comes with the warranty. I am the only author of note that has the effrontery to provide a warranty on all written products. You are the only one that I will confess to that the warranty is useless because the product is equally useless. Substitute nerve for effrontery in the previous sentence to get a more clear meaning.

The revised version of the twelve days of Xmas has been rendered again and is getting pretty greasy. So will slide right on out of here for now. These slopes are getting slipperier _ALL THE TIME_.

_Dby_

12/26/2000

## don belk young

| | |
|---|---|
| **From:** | "don belk young" <donbelk@bellsouth.net> |
| **To:** | "john downey" <jjones2742@aol.com> |
| **Sent:** | Wednesday, December 27, 2000 9:28 AM |
| Subject | NOT MORE THAN FOUR EACH |

This will be hard to do. It is a note that will not have any word with more than four. You can find out four what by use of the gray cell. Or is it grey cell. Keep at it 'til you have it That is the way. See Dick and Jane run. This is dumb. Just like all of them. And that is the way it will be for now and for the rest of the day.

I am okay, just fine. Woo woo is real good and just fine. Yum yum is out and so far so good, so is okay also. Nona is fine, Jeff is OK, with Mike all is well, Mark do all rite; the rest will have to wait cuz name too long.

When we go out, will stay on good road. Bad road not good, so stay off. Will eat at cafe and have wine with meal and call it a gala.

New Year Eve Sun. nite. Have wine Sat nite and Sun nite and Mon, too. Will talk of you and Edie and have wine for you, too, so grin and have fun when we do. Talk of us if you wish but do not tell me or Woo woo if we be bad. Hard to type when use just four you know what. All of them not same, tho, so will try to find a way to stop.

And if you get dere fore I do, just make a hole and pull me thru. That is not all that can be done, but will stop and do over if feel like it some day.

As they say in Two Egg, make mine to go.

12/27/2000

**don belk young**

| | |
|---|---|
| **From:** | "don belk young" <donbelk@bellsouth.net> |
| **To:** | "john downey" <jjones2742@aol.com> |
| **Sent:** | Wednesday, December 27, 2000 10:07 AM |
| **Subject:** | WITH APOLOGIES |

It is not expected that anyone who has the misfortune to have to read the email just sent using words with not then four letters will be arrested for committing a crime against the author. But I do have an excuse. Seldom do I dream about anything and when I do, usually cannot remember what it was about. But last night, in between light sleep and deep, deep snoring, the dream was about whether such an epistle could be done. So that was a shot at it. See, I did it again.

Also dreamed about, it may have been more of a nightmare, the numerical keyboard on the computer and the telephone. The five and the zero are the only digits that you can find in the same place. Otherwise, these conveniences start at different corners of the square of numbers. Wonder why the technical gurus did that! if you can find out, let me know so I can do something with it when it seems appropriate to do so.

My vow for the day is not to trouble you with any of those challenging word discoveries. But have some in reserve that you can look for with an expectant air when future mailings arrive.

The morning paper featured weather in North Little Rock. Probably a good idea to stay out of harm's way, but we never wanted to be there, anyhow.

New issue of Senior Golf magazine came yesterday. Headline on the cover "HOW TO IMPROVE WITHOUT PRACTICE" may be just what we need. Will study that and see whether these same principles can be applied to writing emails, behaving morally, and avoiding stupidity. Now there is what you call a triumvirate if there ever was one.

So once again we come to the signature and with a namaste to each of you, will quietly go away for approximately 24 hours. You will just have to accept our namastes with grace and be assured that you have not been insulted.

12/27/2000

## don belk young

| | |
|---|---|
| **From:** | "don belk young" <donbelk@bellsouth.net> |
| **To:** | "john downey" <jjones2742@aol.com> |
| **Sent:** | Thursday, December 28, 2000 11:03 AM |
| **Subject:** | AND NOW |

Ten o'clock has come and gone and we have already had a full day. You will recall that the most interesting feature of these messages is the vivid description of routine daily procedures that creates an awesome brilliance and brings blinding flashes of insight into full flower. And what we have had today is another example of the enchanting atmosphere that enthralls on a day to day basis. After coffee, etc. we had an opportunity to visit with the pest control guy, fellow named Ernie. He wished us a happy holiday but we had already done that so just chatted amiably about termites and ants until he went cheerfully on his way. Then along came Davis Martin bearing gifts. He brought Woowoo a camera. There is a story about that but do not know how to make it interesting so will not go down that road.

We have just finished a second breakfast of lemon pepper muffins. Best ones we ever had. Only ones we ever had, Quite good. Ought to try it sometime.

Paul Brann called. I had written to him after getting his Arkansas address from Jane. He said that he is having difficulty with eyesight. He lost use of one eye when he had a stroke and has had cataract surgery. Will be in Birmingham on Jan 22 and 23 and we are going to try to get together. Paul mentioned that he was 85.

We have discussed whether we are disgruntled or not, and have reached the conclusion that we am not. Disgruntled that is. So is it logical to conclude that we are gruntled. If so, because we are what is called stoical about this type of thing, we will accept our situation and seek the better things as we pursue life, liberty and happiness, as the pundit opined.

You have mentioned your difficulties with your back. You might want to have your sartorius examined. It is a flat narrow muscle that extends from the hip to the inner thigh and helps rotate the leg to a cross-legged position. It is the longest muscle in the human body. So you can see that you would not want to sprain your sartorius lest it affect your ability to cross your legs and cause backache and other ailments as a result. Parenthetical note: It has been determined through scientific study, statistical analysis, and skillful probing, that women have stronger sartorius muscles than other species, for obvious reasons. End of parentheses.

Have continued the study and research on the twelve days of Christmas. This is day no. 4. Do not want to spoil the thrill of discovery but for the sake of titillation will just say that looking to the twelfth day, when all will be revealed, the leading thought for that day right now is "Twelve twits a twisting." Unless we hear strong objection from somewhere, that will most likely be the opening when all is said and done. You know how that works. When all is said and done, much more will be said than done. And you can write that down. And feel free to use it in your everyday conversations. It is a moral that runs at large, take it, it's free, no extra charge.

On a scale of 1 to 10, my proofreader gave the writings of the 27th a minus 10. So feel free to trash them, but I have a permanent copy on the wall of a cave near Vincent.

Will close today with wit and wisdom. As Albert E. said e is = to itself. I better get outta here.
Dy

12/28/2000

**don belk young**

| | |
|---|---|
| **From:** | "don belk young" <donbelk@bellsouth.net> |
| **To:** | "john downey" <jjones2742@aol.com> |
| **Sent:** | Friday, December 29, 2000 12:16 PM |
| **Subject:** | HUMOR |

A person without a sense of humor is like a wagon without springs—jolted by every pebble in the road. That is a statement of opinion by one of the many philosophers who have come and gone; wonder how those clowns survived the ice age and those well-known crashes like Africa running into North America and creating mountains that came to be known as Appalachia and qualified for a lot of Government aid including the TVA. Then there was the stock market crash of 1929 which some think was the worst of all. The before mentioned and the lesser crashes that have occurred and which I feel sure you can enumerate do indeed test one's ability to see the humor. But it must abound else why would anyone bother to write on walls of caves, not to mention papyrus, etc.

A little travel today. All the way to Columbia, Tennessee. Sarah and Susan will be delighted that we came by with an air hockey game. Scott will be civilized and polite and actually quite likable. Dina will fix anything you would ever want to enjoy victualwise as long as it is macaroni and cheese. We expect the weather to be just dismal enough to make it worth talking about and perhaps test the humor already mentioned. Probably stay over tonight and return tomorrow. Mr. Davis Martin has agreed to accompany us and will probably go to sleep in the middle of a sentence. Woowoo kept him up watching late night television last night but I think they will both have a full recovery in a day or two.

Just got confirmation that men's brains are 15 percent larger than women's. The same report also avers that the corpus callosum—the nerve bundle linking the two hemispheres of the brain and the other two connecting cables, the anterior commissure and the massa intermedia, are significantly larger in women. Surely those findings explain something, probably everything. Reminds me of that proverb—do proverbs invoke stuff—about Volkswagen's. "Anything adjustable will sooner or later need adjustment." That proverb could be used in connection with attitudes, seems to me.

Plodding along here. But to plod is not at all interesting, so, as you are supposed to say just before you get dismissed from your lifelong career job, "I quit."

dy

12/31/2000

**don belk young**

| | |
|---|---|
| **From:** | "don belk young" <donbelk@bellsouth.net> |
| **To:** | "john downey" <jjones2742@aol.com> |
| **Sent:** | Saturday, December 30, 2000 6:13 PM |
| **Subject:** | IT'S HERE SOMEWHERE |

Not enough time to prepare the usual essay with wit, humor and calisthenics of the mind. Must hurry to a UAB basketball game, beginning, to wonder why, so will just list the items that will be thoroughly explained either tomorrow or next day or perhaps, of course, never.

CROSTINI

NASION

IT'S HERE SOMEWHERE

MILEAGE CALCULATIONS

SNOW EXPERIENCE IN TENNESSEE

And whatever else the author might select or receive from that mysterious source commonly referred to as inane, unless opted for by the last part of the first half during the two minute Intermission, assuming back to back recovery of onside kicks. Just relax now. You are not supposed to have the slightest idea what that last sentence was about. And one more thing. Do not ask me anything about it because even if I knew, which I do not, it would be a violation of trust to something or somebody to discuss in a way that makes any sense to you or anyone else, especially you because you have not acquired your present status of zero without a great deal of effort, besides trying real hard.

Got your note. Sorry about the inhospitableness of the hospital, and know that you had some miserable times during the time when most were with family in a comfortable setting. Keep those notes coming and those blood counts rising.

Cheers...................dy..................and..............woowoo!!!!!!!!!!!!!!!!!!!!!

12/30/2000

**don belk young**

| | |
|---|---|
| **From:** | "don belk young" <donbelk@bellsouth.net> |
| **To:** | "john downey" <jjones2742@aol.com> |
| **Sent:** | Sunday, December 31, 2000 11:36 AM |
| **Subject:** | JAN BOOTHE |

Went to the UAB game against VCU last night. Lillian told me that Jan had fallen and had a broken hip. Called Ray just now. He had tried to call while we were in Tennessee but did not leave a message. They had just finished eating at their kitchen table. He went to the bathroom; when he was returning through the den, Jan was walking into the den from the kitchen holding to a wheelchair that she uses. She said to Ray "I'm going to fall" and she did. At the hospital, the doctor said the ball socket was broken; may have broken and caused her to fall, or may have broken when she fell. Replaced the ball socket Friday morning at 6 a.m., she was sitting up yesterday for five hours; plan to go to Rehab hospital Tuesday. When we know more will let you know, of course.

We plan to go to Joe's Ranchhouse tonight. (That does not look right with two h's) You remember that place. it is the one that it only took you a little over an hour to find. But we had a good time anyhow and as someone said "That's what counts."

I promised that you would be enlightened? on the subject of crostini. Suffice it to say that it is best if made one or two days ahead and stored in an airtight container.

The other thing that you were titillated with was naison. And suffice it to say that a naison is the point where the bridge of the nose meets the forehead. At one time it seemed plausible to do something clever by making some connection between crostini and naison but the little gray cell has failed one more time. Experiencing failure enriches the soul, and since enrichment of that type is not as abundant as it should be if we are to save the world, the whales, the redwoods, etc., 1 find it necessary to take all I can get no matter how many failures it takes. So not to worry about who it was that said "The arrow you dropped will be collected by someone else." Ovambo be damned. I am going to take a great risk and quote Dave Barry who has quoted Benjamin Franklin about GETTING ORGANIZED. The pithy maxim goes thus "if a man be organized, then that man be a lot more organized than the man whom do not be as organized as the first man I was talking about earlier in this maxim." Had to get that in there to demonstrate that Barry (and we are not talking Barry Switzer here) has now began to emulate this author in an attempt to get recognition for inanity, unerudition, and just plain silliness.

And about mileage calculations which was also listed as a subject for enlightenment. That will have to wait because the base number of ten is temporarily out of service.

And on that uplifting note, please say hello and smile at a stranger. But do not a stranger be.

May the wind always be in your face. It will keep you awake and probably save you from a disaster.
ww/dy et al


P.S. UAB won 70-61.


12/31/2000

**don belk young**

| | |
|---|---|
| **From:** | "don belk young" <donbelk@bellsouth.net> |
| **To:** | "john downey" <jjones2742@aol.com> |
| **Sent:** | Monday, January 01, 2001 11:39 AM |
| **Subject:** | 2001 |

Sure enough the new millennium is here. We managed to see the New Year begin in both New York and Birmingham, Were at our other friend's house (we were at your place last year) last night and did the TV watching properly with after dinner drinks and a real wood fire in the fireplace. John, I need your counsel. Is it proper for me to go out on New Year's Eve with three, yes, three, beautiful women. They have assorted backgrounds but are well respected as far as I know, so no concern in that regard. But how Is one to behave in those circumstances. There was never a hint of play or tussle, not a one of us moved a muscle (not even the sartorius, really), except to poke the fire or lift the glass. Any advice would be appreciated for a minute or two and then probably forgotten forever. I have really been working on this forgetting business and have almost got it worked out.

A little snow this morning. But no problems with traveling nor any continuing storm—the sun is shining. Must do the bowl game watching, of course. Later today the Young clan will try to be in the same place at the same time for a little while. Cynthia has arrived from Memphis by way of North Georgia and Atlanta so we will have a bit of family Christmas on the 7th day of Christmas. Five more to go and you will be the recipient of the long awaited Twelve Days of Xmas which has been personalized just for you.

Speaking of snow. it was mentioned in the previous paragraph if you need a point of reference. The trip to Columbia, Tennessee was revelatory in ways that were astounding. It really wasn't that big a deal except for the discovery of a couple of hills previously uncharted. A secondary road not heavily traveled that day (Friday) was covered with snow and ice. With an experienced snow driver at the wheel, we did not become hysterical—more like scared half to death—when the car started slipping and did not go forward. It went backward. The previously mentioned experienced snow driver did exactly what an experienced snow driver is supposed to do, let the car go wherever the hell it wants to go. So backwards we go. And back and back until we were as far back as we could go because a peekup truck was about three feet from the back bumper and was not going to go any farther back for one simple reason. He could not go back any further. (Is it farther or further?) So with due deliberation and resolution, carefully controlled the speed and rpm to derive just the right amount of momentum to reach the top of the slippery slope. And guess what! There was another slippery slope just like the one just surmounted. So we discovered two previously uncharted hills in a couple of minutes. Davis won on his Gameboy machine during this thrilling ascent. The rest of the trip was anticlimactic and uneventful except for backing into the driveway, but you probably do not want to know about that.

If I can find a George Will piece that was around here somewhere, will use it to plagiarize an unknown author about unknowns, some of which are known and others are not known, or unknown.

Hoping you find it impossible to put this down without a complete reading at one time, we are gone for now.

Happy millennium to you, Eydie. We love you and hope that your slightest wish for 2001 is gratified tenfold.

ww/dy

01/01/2001

**don belk young**

| | |
|---|---|
| **From:** | "don belk young" <donbelk@bellsouth.net> |
| **To:** | "john downey" <jjones2742@aol.com> |
| **Sent:** | Tuesday, January 02, 2001 2:33 PM |
| **Subject:** | IT SEEMED LIKE THE THING TO DO AT THE TIME |

Do not have anything to report, so will carry on as usual since meaningful thoughts and ideas are not required in the process of transferring random thought sequences to the papyrus through the keyboard. It used to be called typing a letter but that expression has such an ordinary sound that it must be something else. As indicated in the subject, it seemed like the thing to do at the time. Fellow we know uses that every time he gets caught in an exaggeration, more commonly called lying. Always try to get hold of a mitigating circumstance when you are snared by your own petard. Read about one really mean person, may have been an ogre, who kept mitigating until he was convinced that he was a victim and just walked away.

The wisdom and astute observations made in these conversations have usually been credited to somebody. Anyone can have them and it would be alright with me. Anonymous gets his share. I say his because I never heard of a female anonymous. It occurs to me that that would be what you call an omnibus, you know, one of those expressions that seems to contradict itself, like legal brief, etc. There are a lot of those things out there. Anyhow the scientific community has independently determined that it is impossible for a female to be anonymous. And I am unanimous in that. On the other hand—Harry Truman said he needed a one armed economist so he could not forever be saying "on the other hand"—another very effective way to avoid responsibility is to opine that you received the information "on good authority." Here you must be careful. Good authority is a rare commodity and no one has access to an unlimited supply, so use carefully and in an erudite a way as you can. Using that technique, and others that will be revealed to you at an appropriate time, you will be able to go forward at full speed without any idea where you are going. The best part is that you also do not know where you have been, so cannot be held accountable for anything bad that has ever occurred whilst being very modest about the myriad of accomplishments that you are accoladed for lo these many years. When all else fails, tell the dog story.

It may be about time for a disclaimer, so I take this opportunity to disclaim, i.e., excuse myself for using facts that do not exist and for making up the truth when it does not exist either. Surely you can see the de facto wisdom here. If you think something has been left out, just wait 'til you see the latest edition of a future edition that will require a double disclaimer. The Pope said it was more than he could handle at this time. He was having trouble with arthritis and a couple of fallen angels and just wanted to have a glass of wine and take a nap.

A cousin of obtuse is otiose. Not really, but has a certain alliteration, don't you think. Otiose is the same as worthless, with no useful result or practical purpose.

And that does it for now.

dy


01/02/2001

**don belk young**

From:          "don belk young" &lt;donbelk@bellsouth.net&gt;
To:             "john downey" &lt;jjones2742@aol.com&gt;
Sent:          Wednesday, January 03, 2001 4:00 PM
Subject:     FAME AT LAST

As has been mentioned many times in these discussions, sooner or later something will surely happen to justify the meaningless, seemingly, ramblings that have been running rampant here. One of my readers was so impressed with not being able to comprehend or make any sense out any of the numerous incomprehensible writings. So the only logical thing to do was to send a copy to, guess who, a lawyer. It is well known that lawyers have been trained to make sense out of those issues that no one else can find a place to start, and, this is vital, they also have been trained to do it the other way around, i.e. render those things that are absolutely certain into a useless hodgepodge of uncertainties and misinformation. It must have become quite noticeable that this has become an obsession for both the reader and the readee. My publisher has taken the liberty—he had to take it, I sure was not going to give him or her or anyone else any of my liberties—and has encouraged me to stop as soon as I can without suffering serious withdrawal problems, probably a sentence at a time but as you can see the tendency to indulge in rambling, run on sentences and paragraphs, not to mention a clause or two now and then has taken on its own identity known and understood only by others with the same kind of talent, so it is obvious that there is not very many of them and they propagate just like everybody else in what appears to be a successful attempt to preserve the status of something.

It has without a doubt been a long time since you or any of your loyal followers have been subjected to such a blatant attempt to intimidate them.

As Pythagoras said "intimidated people always say they are not intimidated; that's the nature of intimidation." But here is the really good one by, of course, anonymous "No one should grow old who isn't prepared to be ridiculous." I am ready, as you can see. Or can you.

The vehicle we are now using for driving lessons for yours truly has a feature that displays how many miles you can go until you have gone as far as you can go. It works on the principle that we developed in your martini lab a few moons ago. Suppose it reads 200 when you look at it, then a mile later it will read 199. The car also has an odometer, commonly called a speedometer by the unschooled, which measures mileage in a forward manner. Suppose it reads 200 when you look at it then a mile later it will read 201. Well, while returning from Columbia, Tennessee last Saturday, the party of the first part went from 200 to 95, which comes out right near 105. At the same time, the party of the second part went from 200 to 335, which is about 135. So when you return to your laboratory would you please work this out for all of us in some logical manner. If you would prefer it would certainly be plausible, using the GTP (General Theory of Plausibility), for me to make up a story to prove this in whatever direction you want to go. Please advise. New, tell you what, really do not want to know.

The word of the day is revanche. it is a policy of reclaiming territory, which reminds me that I must be diligent in this respect because I have lost a lot of territory, especially in the last 38 days.

Two days to go when all will be revealed in the Twelve Days of Xmas message. It is scheduled to occur at that time because that is the twelfth day of Christmas.

As the onetime king of Egypt is said to have said ............Tut, tut.

01/03/2001

**don belk young**

| | |
|---|---|
| **From:** | "don belk young" <donbelk@bellsouth.net> |
| **To:** | "john downey" <jjones2742@aol.com> |
| **Sent:** | Thursday, January 04, 2001 10:07 AM |
| **Subject:** | AND THE SAME TO YOU BUSTER |

Like almost everyone, including the animals, some days are better than others, and sometimes you can't tell the difference unless you look for it and face up to a couple of shortcomings (can you have a longcoming) and just proceed from there. So that is the theme today.

A common shortcoming, speaking thereof, is mundanicity, which means to be mundane. This seemingly innocuous personal defect cannot be duplicated exactly and is not contagious so not to worry if you have a small amount The last time I had a small amount of something was a very short time back when we had a gray cell count and we only had about six trillion left. Each of these memos uses about a half million, and the bad news here is that some of them are replaceable and some are not but you never know until suddenly you do not have any. I think it will be OK as long as cholesterol stays below 200 and women continue in their nurturing role. Does nurturing include household duties like taking out the garbage? We may deal with that in a future scientific study.

The prospect of returning to the golf course tomorrow looks good. Our lake was ice filled again this morning but the sun is shining and temperature is supposed to go to the mid 40's, then 50 degrees for the weekend, which we have already started. John & Eydie, wish we could email homemade chili and bread pudding. As the philosopher known as Plato but who was really Eastwood, it would make your day. You know that nee is a word used to explain that somebody used to have a different name, so you might say, I suppose, Eastwood nee Plato, which would make it perfectly clear if it did not make any difference anyhow. Try yclept.

UAB managed to win last night 76-68 but tried one more time to make it interesting by wasting a good lead during the second half. Next is Tulane at 8:30 Sunday night. Must be a TV game for a schedule like that

Tomorrow is the big day that you have been eagerly looking forward to, so no matter what you think about it, you are required to acknowledge that the Twelve Day thing is an epic. An epic is an abbreviated hiccup according to Hoyle but we are not playing poker here (remember that three of a kind beats two pair—says so on that card in your shirt pocket) so think of these writings in a positive way and forward them to both of your friends without requesting advance approval.

Buster was my best friend for 18 years, so let us think positive thoughts in this season of mercy and forgiveness. Besides you cannot blame Attila the Hun for the Fall of Rome because he wasn't anywhere near there at the time. But for some reason the Romans said the Huns were not human, which was only partly true. As in any other group of people, including animals, some of them were human and some were not.

And so we find it necessary to get out of here in a hurry.          dy

You are indeed ENTITLED to a _____ Fill in the blank with an eight letter word.

01/04/2001

**don belk young**

| | |
|---|---|
| **From:** | "don belk young" <donbelk@bellsouth.net> |
| **To:** | "john downey" <jjones2742@aol.com> |
| **Sent:** | Friday, January 05, 2001 11:02 AM |
| **Subject:** | MEDITATION, MAYBE |

To meditate or not to meditate, that is the question. It is also a soliloquy, I think. But I have decided not to meditate because if you meditate and something bad happens like spilling your bonnyclabber or a murder, then it is called premeditation and a presumption of guilt and a lot of bad things can happen because one meditated. If William S. had the benefit of advice from an old sage like you, bet he would never have soliloquized about meditation or meditated about soliloquies. Thus we have reached a conflicting conclusion compounded by carefully crafted and convoluted coercive certainties culminating in a cocky attitude.

(To alleviate your presumed perplexity about the meaning of bonnyclabber, It is called blinky, or sour milk, in places like Little Rack, Coffeen, and Mountain Brook.)

Received your email about Eydie's continued improvement and will have an extra cup of coffee to celebrate. And was pleased to see that you look forward to the daily diversion, those carefully crafted nonsensicals. Today, of course, is the twelfth day we have all been waiting for. I really do not know how this is going to work out but hero goes.

On the twelfth day of Christmas, Eydie sent to me-
TWELVE TWITS A TWISTING
Eleven lemmas lemming
TEN LITTLE GRAY CELLS
Nine erudite email soliloquies

EIGHT EPIPHANIES
Seven serendipities
SIX SACKS OF ROMONTADE
Five Jersey cows
WITH FOUR TEATS EACH
a Three legged milk stool
TWO DOGS A SNIFFING
And a one egg pudding for me

Perhaps you need footnote explanations about teats. That word was not used to avoid using a more titillating term like tits, it was used because it is the correct term for those appendages on all female cows from which the milk of the day comes on a daily basis. Besides that is what my Dad called them. You may be interested in knowing that the first time I ever saw one was when I was six weeks old. Another little known fact is that I squeezed, let's see if I can figure this out. For twelve years, from 1930 until 1942, milked eight cows each day. Each cow has four teats. Each teat must be squeezed 41 times to complete the milking task. So twelve times 365 = 4380 days times 8 = 27040 times 32 (4x8) = 865,280 teats squeezed times 41 squeezes each = total squeeze count of 35,476,480. Lest we be accused of spurious accuracy here, round out to 36 million.

And at the risk of belaboring the titillation, ta ta and tut tut.

01/05/2001

**don belk young**

| | |
|---|---|
| **From:** | "don belk young" <donbelk@bellsouth.net> |
| **To:** | "john downey" <jjones2742@aol.com> |
| **Sent:** | Saturday, January 06, 2001 11:19 AM |
| **Subject:** | TOO CLEVER BY HALF |

John and Eydie, hope I did not promise to be clever today, or even too clever by half, whatever that means, because I can tell without even thinking about it, which is a rare occurrence, that it is just not in the tarots today. But not to worry. We are not going to do another classic like the Twelve Days thing, or even calculating teat squeezings.

A note about Jan. We may have told you by telephone. Alter replacement of the broken bone in the hip, she is now at Spain Rehabilitation Hosp. and has, I think, a two hour session twice a day as part of the rehab process. Ray seemed equally concerned about her mental abilities; says she just stares sometimes and he does not know whether they are communicating or not. We think she must have had a stroke during all this. It has been about a year since she has been active at all.

In case you missed the reference to Buster, it occurs to me that it went largely unexplained, which is not the usual outcome of these sentences where each thought is carefully thought of before it is committed to paper for anyone else to think about. Anyhow, Buster was a horse that had the same birthday as several other horses, but he was different. How could you have the name Buster and not be different. So when I was two years old and so was Buster, my Dad introduced us and he was my riding companion for the next sixteen years. The only reason I used a saddle was to have a place to hang the water jugs. That's what Buster and I did, mostly. Carried water to the workers in the wheat field in the summertime. The gallon jugs had a corncob for a stopper; everyone drank directly from the jug so the guy who was chewing tobacco had to drink last for obvious reasons; no ice within ten miles so did not have that complication; and we always pulled the water bucket out of the well from the north side where the water was cooler. Right after I went off to win WWII Buster died of a broken heart. I thought that I had been zigzwanged—that is a situation in which one is forced into making a disadvantageous move and involves considerable risk, including a chance of being misunderstood.

John, I know you are a gourmand, i.e. you have an appreciation of good food and drink, so will send the recipe for bread pudding tomorrow in which the recipe will be cleverly disguised as another of those daily notes entitled BREAD PUDDING.

So do the best you can until then, and as Haile Selassie would say, Abyssinia, like in I'll be seein' ya.

01/06/2001

## don belk young

| | |
|---|---|
| **From:** | "don belk young" <donbelk@bellsouth.net> |
| **To:** | "john downey" <jjones2742@aol.com> |
| **Sent:** | Sunday, January 07, 2001 11:41 AM |
| **Subject:** | BREAD PUDDING |

**Bread pudding is not something you decide to do. It is a random act of kindness that occurs every once in awhile, sort of at random. But you can do this every day if you want to. You need a loaf of raisin bread and two cans of condensed milk. The best part of all is that it is not a one egg pudding. Use four eggs. You can beat these and you can beat your dog and you can beat your wife but you can't beat a good game of golf. Fooled you there, didn't we. That entire recipe is around here somewhere and will send it on, probably.**

*Eydie was inquiring about those unusual words that have somehow crept into these messages. There is a story about that which 1 may feel free to divulge at an appropriate time and in the right circumstances. One of my first experiences using words that had not been fully explained was when I told a young lady with whom was having a scholarly discussion that I would not mollycoddle her. Her response was that she would like very much for me to do so. So I did. Later she admitted that she did not know what it meant, either, but that she had a good time and that it seemed like the thing to do at the time. I told her that my Mom would consider her to be a trollop and she said thank you very much and mollycoddled me right back. This happened to me at a very impressionable age and has obviously contributed to my delinquency in several ways which I would articulate about but only with permission which is not likely to be forthcoming.*

The UAB game is on ESPN2 at 8:30. At home vs. Tulane. Hope the TV cameras do not show any crowd scenes because there probably won't be any—

crowd, I mean. AD Frazier has some work to do to get customers. Probably all he needs is a winning team.

John, you are not known as a historian except for your knowledge about the origin of dog sniffing. But I would recommend "The Decline and Fail of Practically Everybody" by Will Cuppy. it was published in 1950 before Congress put a number on every book so you may not be able to find it in any library. A sample. "Egyptians of the First Dynasty were civilized in most respects. They had hieroglyphics, metal weapons for killing foreigners, numerous government officials, death, and taxes. They invented mosquito netting, astrology, and a calendar that wouldn't work. They believed that the sun went sailing around Egypt on a boat, and that a pig ate the moon every two weeks."

But let's do the bread pudding. Here it is. One recipe for the pudding, another for the sauce.

> Pudding ingredients are: 12 raisin bread slices; 1 14oz can Eagle brand condensed milk; 3/4 cup hot water; 4 large eggs; 2 tsp vanilla; 1/4 tsp ground cinnamon; 1/4 tsp nutmeg;
>
> Set oven temp at 350. Lightly grease 8" square dish. Tear bread into pieces and put into dish.
>
> In a bowl, stir together milk and next five items (beat eggs), pour over bread pieces, place dish in large pan. Add hot water to pan to depth of 1". Bake for 35-40 min. or 'til knife comes out clean.
>
> Prepare sauce. Heat one can 14oz Eagle condensed milk and 1/4 cup butter until butter melts. Remove from heat and stir in 1/3 cup bourbon (go ahead, use 1/2 cup) and 1 tsp vanilla. Serve pudding warm. Pour warm sauce over pudding. Leftovers can be microwaved.

The recipe was intentionally typed in small type and placed in the middle of the page so you can make a copy of this most important message and cut and paste the recipe on a 3x5 card.

Enjoy. If you do not have the inclination to fool with it, will make some with your name on it when you are next around these parts, which we hope will be soon. dy

01/07/2001

## don belk young

| | |
|---|---|
| **From:** | "don belk young" <donbelk@bellsouth.net> |
| **To:** | "john downey" <jjones2742@aol.com> |
| **Sent:** | Monday, January 08, 2001 12:44 PM |
| **Subject:** | THE FIRST TIME |

John, do you remember the first time. You should be thinking the first time what. If you are that would be a normal thing to do. And, as we all know, you are very normal except for your obsession for going to the mailbox for your highlight of the day. However, upon reflection, that may be normal and the rest of us are something else. But back to the first time. What I remember about the first time more than anything is where it was and who it was with. This is sort of personal and confidential so will have to think about it while proceeding and may be comfortable with complete and full disclosure at a later time.

UAB had a great game last night. For the audience of ESPN2 it should have been entertaining if they had never heard of Ala-Birm. The highlight of the first half was a Tulane guard making four consecutive three shots; he was four for five at half time and UAB was ahead by just one point. Then the second half began and UAB was in control all the way. Two of their players made six three point shots during this time and both teams played a good game. It was really good when it was over with the score 98-76 in favor of UAB.

We went to Silvertron Cafe before the game, which did not begin until 8:30. It was raining most of the time, but despite the weather, late starting time, and so-so record of both teams, was probably the best crowd of the year. Bob Glaze asked if we had heard from you and we told them that Eydie was at the apartment now and going for daily evaluations and treatment Don Griffin told us that Harvey Smith is in a hospice facility, not doing very well at all. Nancy Stewart is recovering from a heart attack. Ray and Jan were not there, of course.

I think I am having an attack of torpor, a lack of mental energy. But never fear we shall overcome. Some well-known philosopher said that once upon a time, must have been Thutmose, who tried to remove all reference to his Aunt Hatshepsut by chopping the noses off her statues which were mostly in the form of an obelisk, dumped the statues into a deep quarry, walled up her best obelisk, and tried to erase the hieroglyphics on the walls of almost everything. It didn't work, of course, and you can go the Metropolitan Museum of Art to look at these statues even now.

I must be having an aftermath, which is the consequence of an event, especially a disastrous one. But we not had any genuine disasters for a day or so. Will have to go unexplained for now. When the gray cells come back will take another look.

Further thought about the first time. What it was was the first time I ever heard of a weather channel.

Fascinating to discover that such an ordinary day to day thing could be so important that a TV station would talk about it all the time. And where was I. That is probably not a proper sentence but not to worry, the discussion is about the first time to see a weather channel, not what is or is not a proper sentence. And where did this remarkable event occur? That's better. I was in the den/TV room at the Boothe residence. They had a new TV with cable service and there it was. And now you know the rest of the story.

The malaise which caused torpor resulting in aftermath may have occurred because I have not had my daily working the crossword fix. So will adjourn this session and work toward a full recovery.

What is a two letter word for a three toed sloth. We may never know.

Ciao

01/08/2001

## don belk young

| | |
|---|---|
| **From:** | "don belk young" <donbelk@bellsouth.net> |
| **To:** | "john downey" <jjones2742@aol.com> |
| **Sent:** | Tuesday, January 09, 2001 12:22 PM |
| **Subject:** | WHELMED AGAIN |

I have just had a lifestyle altering experience but think it might be best to try to ignore it in case there are some serious consequences. Will give you a full and complete unabridged report when it seems like the thing to do.

About first lime stuff. Had another one of those today. Ordered a supply of checks from the Credit Union by email. It was a real thrill but will surely be forgotten in a day or two.

Also, have used most of the morning in an analytical mode. Michael had a file of info about a bank loan that would defy meaningful analysis to ordinary people (there must be some average people somewhere) but when subjected to my insight those otherwise bland meaningless documents revealed their contents in a meaningful way. So you can plainly see that it was much more than say, adding 2+2. Actually, the answer was 21361.34 and they are called dollars and sense. There is a subtle double entendre right there. Wonder what a single entendre is. If we could discuss in a scholarly manner, probably could determine the meaning and significance. But as you know, any subject that arises in connection with or as a result of these writings is not dealt with unless it is more important than something else. And if Eydie thinks that it is supposed to have a hidden meaning she is absolutely right. All will be revealed at some future time. In this context, please realize that we are still finding out about things that happened billions of years ago, so in another billion years or so the real meaning of this email and other recent editions may be revealed. The cave writings near Vincent will probably be deciphered much sooner.

Have ran out of clever ways to say sayonara so you can do this one any way you want to... dy

01/09/2001

## don belk young

| From: | "don belk young" <donbelk@bellsouth.net> |
|---|---|
| To: | "john downey" <jjones2742@aol.com> |
| Sent: | Wednesday, January 10, 2001 11:04 AM |
| Subject: | RX |

The day started as a golf day and will be later. We must wait for the frost to go away. And there are some other considerations which are so complicated that even though 1 have a complete and thorough understanding of these matters, and have great talents to make such complications understandable to ordinary people, just do not have the verve and passion required to indulge in such elementary matters at this time. Besides, I do not want to and that is all the reason needed. Since I learned the lessons of life by the dim and flickering light of a wood fire in an otherwise cold house with a dirt floor and a stone hearth that froze your tongue if you touched it, I use my talents sparingly lest they be consumed in the course of everyday events when they need to be reserved for use in urgent situations. As one of my contemporaries—have forgotten his name but his initials are John Jones—was said to have said "you have earned the right to be eccentric," so let's just call it that.

The RX title in the subject line refers to an experience that I have just successfully completed. The health cartel thought that they could change the rules and arbitrarily impose a higher fee for my Zocor prescription. Again, I know that you know all about Zocor because you told me so. After diligent follow-up regarding how come the stuff cost $85, it took only seven phone calls, and approximately 2 hours and six minutes to get it resolved to my satisfaction. Will now use Upitor which will cost $15 for a ninety day supply of 20 milligram tablets. If I was burdened with an 'A' personality, probably would have failed completely to get resolved and would be taking blood pressure medicine. Just isn't worth it. I may have mentioned that you should not sweat the small stuff, etc.

Came across the term ribaldry recently. Do not think I have had any of that, at least not for a long time, May experiment with just a little bit at a time to determine my capacity for such We had a little practice last night at Lovoy's. Had an opportunity to use the dog story. The people we were with did not know why dogs do what they do, so it was necessary to tell the story and was very effective in providing further documentation that my thought processes sometimes work and sometimes they do not. Actually, it was questioned openly after my rendition of the story so we blamed it on you. Said that had quoted you directly and that if they did not understand it or, gasp, did not appreciate the wit and humor, not to mention the droll hang dog expression, that they should go home and feed their own dogs. So they did.

Have you ever been called an old geezer. I do not want to be the first to congratulate you on achieving such status. But if you do qualify, there is an Internet address you might want to check out. It is thegeezerbrigade.com. I intend to look it up when this note is finished, but my email system sends this as soon as it is finished so it will be sent before I have been able to evaluate it. There is some risk here that it is worthless, but as long as it you wasting your time and not mine, it is clear that the less valuable time is being wasted. Have you ever been insulted so many times in such a droll manner?

As they say under certain circumstances...........................FORE!!!!!!!!!!!

dy

01/10/2001

## don belk young

| From: | "don belk young" <donbelk@bellsouth.net> |
| To: | "john downey" <jjones2742@aol.com> |
| Sent: | Thursday, January 11, 2001 10:37 AM |
| Subject: | BREAD PUDDING REVISITED |

Let's hear it for Eydie May Gamble. The only reader with the candor to challenge this writer with a mistake. Of course that did not occur since it has been determined that such never happens from this keyboard. Nevertheless, however it occurred, one omission needs to be put into place so that it is no longer missing. Immediately after the word pour on line 5 of the recipe for bread pudding add the word over. The missing word technique is a writing technique to measure the alertness of the readership and we appreciate the opportunity to acknowledge that Miss Eydie gets the prize for this one. And if you have any other questions please hesitate to ask because you would get the same answer and would be subject to a psychological risk of acquiring so much self-esteem that you would be assigned to some elitist coterie and suffer Napoleonitis. That is sometimes referred to as exile which occurred on the island of Elba, according to most historical accounts. I do not believe that because historians do not have a very good record of getting it right. Examples supplied upon request. If we can't find any, the little gray cells will think of something.

Speaking of LGC (little gray cells) we are experiencing an onslaught of alliteration, (Have you noticed the use of the editorial we? It is a proven method that creates confusion about who is really responsible for idiotic utterances and writings and provides the proverbial cya, not to mention anonymity.) Pour over the bread pieces. Then say without taking a breath "pour the porridge into the proper portal to portray propriety and proportion to proactive protagonists and proceed to prolong any preference you prefer." This will cause you to forget almost everything if you have not already done so.

Was accused of being corrigible in the recent past. Will make a serious attempt to get the "in" restored in front of corrigible. Based on events that have taken place over the last 72 years—can't remember what happened before I started milking cows—this restoration will occur within the next 24 hours. I have never gone a full day without some amount of incorrigibility. It's a burden that you learn to live with. It is something you do when others are arrogant, stubborn and aggressive; a way to be yourself and watch with bemused amusement the chaos so characteristic of that class of people who just cannot cope with everyday happenings, like dealing with gallinippers. Unless you put a gallinipper in its place, it will bedevil you with pain and suffering so I say smash them with a fly swatter, and if the blood splatters clean it up. I think that came out right although I am not using the azerty. That is the European version of the qwerty keyboard. Bet you did not know that.

Surely you are not astonished by anything so far. You should be inured? to excursions into the unknown by the LGC, since they have demonstrated consistently that anything can happen. As one of the lesser known philosophers was said to have said "use your inclination as long as it does not lead you anywhere." This will keep you from reaching your potential which most of us should not even consider. if you did not know, you can accept this wisdom from the LGC. Most potentials never happen. If you think about it, a potential is not one if it happens.

Again, we have crossed the line without having scored. I thought about apologizing but could not see how that would bring closure and you would not believe it anyhow. So to hell with it. And I am unanimous in that.

Pretend that you hear background music fading away and a sunset described by a poet laureate and you will experience once again the great relief that comes with finishing one of these and wondering what was that all about.

Adios, amigo and amiga (amiga is the feminine of amigo, thought you needed to know).

01/22/2001

**don belk young**

| | |
|---|---|
| **From:** | "don belk young" <donbelk@bellsouth.net> |
| **To:** | "john downey" <jjones2742@aol.com> |
| **Sent:** | Friday, January 12, 2001 5:09 PM |
| **Subject:** | ANOTHER WEEKEND UNDERWAY |

Another gloomy winter day. It seemed like the sun was shining from about 9 a.m. until 1 p.m. while we were at the golf course. That was the propaganda of the day until we got back to the clubhouse with frozen digits—you know, toes and such. And it has taken me until 5 p.m. to recover sufficiently to attempt the keyboard skills one more time. The LGC are somnambulant also so we are going rather slow, about 50 wpm.

Wake for Harvey Smith is at St. Peter's this evening. He was 82. I think I mentioned before that they had not been to any games this year. We have another visitation this evening also at Ridout's. Virginia Lester, a lady that went to New Hope Cumberland Church and we had been good friends for about thirty years.

So must take a timeout and will resume later this evening.

01/13/2001

## don belk young

| | |
|---|---|
| **From:** | "don belk young" <donbelk@bellsouth.net> |
| **To:** | "john downey" <jjones2742@aol.com> |
| **Sent:** | Saturday, January 13, 2001 12:09 PM |
| **Subject:** | GREMLINS |

We found so many gremlins and executed them by the millions that I thought they might have gone the dinosaur route. That is where they turn to oil, then the Arabs dig it up and turn it into gold and put it into a secret account in a Swiss bank. That is the one sentence history of the world, according to some. But at least one gremlin showed up yesterday and sent that unfinished email before it was finished. Then first one thing and then two or three others, like sloth and laziness, not to mention general malaise and a bad attitude and the first thing you know I just let the gremlin have his (or her) way with me and never looked back. Sure enough nothing was following.

About that alliterative altercation the other day. Did you think anything was left out of the one involving a lot of words that started with pro. Professionally I thought that both the protuberance and the prosthesis was missing until it became that the protuberance was a prosthesis. So thought it should not be redone. If it is OK with you, it will only be mentioned again upon receipt of a petition of at least two or three persons with credentials that cannot be challenged.

Eydie, the School of Optometry has put into place a stealth plan to steal UAB. Dan Osborn has been named associate provost for administration and finance for the University. I can remember when he was only an accountant, but I know his father-in-law. Ed Gregg was the internal auditor at UAB and knows where the skeletons are, including those in the anatomy lab. So it only logical to assume that Dan has a mission to become even more influential. If you know anything about this nefarious undertaking, please do not tell me. You can tell John because by the time he goes to the mailbox a couple of times he will not remember anything that has happened lately unless he wants to.

Be patient. We are waiting for a random flash of brilliance, a spark that will result in a continuance of the theme that has been so carefully cultivated. Almost had it but it got away. One thing that is a certainty, Friday the 13th came on Saturday this month. One problem with recognition of the presence of a brilliant idea is that the LGC are doing teraflops most of the time. They hardly ever take a time out. A teraflop is the speed of info transmission and in particular means one trillion thoughts per second. I expect you will think you have missed a few teraflops somewhere along the way, but it may be a good thing to not have to deal with all of that at one time. The more things you attempt to deal with at the same time, you more likely you are to budge.

Hiss and Buzz are two common words that need no additional explanation. But the origin of them are of interest to scholars everywhere because they are representative of a process that could not, be pronounced or spelled until very recently when I was fortunate enough to capture one of those teraflops at its peak. And I feel comfortable revealing this revelation to you because truly believe that you will not give it any consideration at all, which is what you are supposed to do when you do not know the answer but want to act like you do. The process is onomatopoeia and that is the last word on that.

Can you sneeze with your eyes open. You cannot. But if you have singultus, aka hiccups, there are more ways to overcome them than there are fathers. That is because there are more mothers than there are fathers and each mother has a cure for singultus. Just ask anyone and they will tell you whether you asked or not what their mother did for hiccups. There have been two validated cases of mothers who did not know the answer and they were later determined to be malleus malefecarums, witches. A footnote: They knew the answer, also, but lied about it because it was not something that they wanted to waste any time with.

Surely this has developed into a genuine diversion. if not, pretend. We are saving valetudinarian for future discussion.

We will take another risk this evening in connection with the UAB game vs. Southern Miss. The risk has become known around here as the Davis/Caleb connection. These two almost eight-year-olds are just like any other two people. When they are alone, they behave somewhat normally and do not require a large amount of supervision. When they are together, the energy level increases geometrically and requires somewhat more skillful application of disciplinary action, Since I can obtain any skill that is needed upon short notice, it may become necessary to use some of my reserves, The good part of all that is that such skills are renewable. In other words, just because you have yelled and screamed a few times does not mean that you cannot continue to do so. And if Davis can get a hot dog without anything on it he will settle down for two or three minutes. He has all the instincts to be a solid conservative by the time he reaches his 4oth birthday; that when most adults become adults and experience their first epiphany. A similar evaluation about Caleb must await further evaluation (redundancy intended).

*TRIED TO THINK OF A LIMERICK OR TWO, TO CLOSE THIS AMUSING AND AMAZING REVUE BUT THE TERAFLOP FLOPPED AND MY GLC STOPPED. AND THEN MY SNEEZE SAID ACHOO.*

If that is not a goodbye for now Just assume that it is.

01/13/2001

**don belk young**

| | |
|---|---|
| **From:** | "don belk young" <donbelk@bellsouth.net> |
| **To:** | "john downey" <jjones2742@aol.com> |
| **Sent:** | Sunday, January 14, 2001 3:48 PM |
| **Subject:** | SANGUINITY |

This one will need to write itself, since I do not know anything about sanguine. I have heard scholars like Bob Glaze use it but never could make a direct connection to its real meaning. I never heard you speak thusly so you must not be a scholar. If you wish to demur, I do know what that means. Demurrage is when something is deducted from you because you did not fix something that you did not know was in heed of being fixed. It has to come from somewhere and you were chosen to have it happen to you. May look into that more deeply soon. Did not come out quite right.

UAB had another bad night. Lost to Southern Miss. Did not look good at all in the first half—made a total of 15 points. Will be at Cincinnati and Tulane before playing at Bartow Arena again on the 24th. Speaking of Bartow, Athletic Director Emeritus was at the game last night and was as useful as he always is. You can make that out anyway you want to.

Pretty exciting around here today. A Brownie came by to sell Girl Scout cookies; spilled the bread pudding on the kitchen floor; Michael borrowed the drill; New York Giants gave Minnesota lessons on how to play football; AND went to the mailbox to send the monthly Discover premium (will get a $14 refund from that one in August, can hardly wait); AND have gone down the seventeen steps 17 times and up the seventeen steps 16 times, so as you can see I am upstairs right now. You could have arrived at that conclusion in a couple other ways, but you got it right the first time so no need to drone on and on about non-essential trivia. On the other hand, why not. It fills up space and keeps up the suspense about when one might see something here that is truly meaningful. So pay attention. You might find the explanation about Tallahassee in the middle of a paragraph so would not recommend skip reading. Or you might miss one of those priceless limerick things. They must be priceless. No one ever transferred any assets to me for a single one.

So me and Buster go riding off into the sunset one more time. ..........dy

01/14/2001

**don belk young**

| | |
|---|---|
| **From:** | "don belk young" <donbelk@bellsouth.net> |
| **To:** | "john downey" <jjones2742@aol.com> |
| **Sent:** | Monday, January 15, 2001 117 PM |
| **Subject:** | MORE THAN GLAD |

You know it is Monday when you call for a tee time and AVCC is closed. Also, we got your note and it was dated January 15. When we looked at that date in 2001, sure enough it was Monday. So we are going to celebrate in some appropriate way. Actually, we are more than glad to participate in whatever is a good way to celebrate as long as it is not difficult. We have never experienced a difficult celebration. But back to the phrase *more than glad*. Do you know when it is appropriate to say that you will be more than glad to do something. How is that possible? Why would it not be more correct to say that you would be elated to do that? Since you do not know, I will reveal the secret. The reason it is not correct to say that you will be elated to do something is that it just does not sound right. You must trust your ear. That leads to another conundrum. Can one trust ones ears? In my experience, my ears are not always trustworthy as a transmitter of things that have been said. I have been known to not hear things that have been clearly transmitted, and have been heard by others within earshot. Have gone astray here, so if you have a theory about why the phrase *more than glad* has become quite common as a way of just saying something when you cannot think of anything else. And what about earshot. It sounds inhumane.

In my daily research today, my sources indicate that this writer deserves a zindabad because my zines have been successful. To expand for your edification a zindabad is a loud shout of approval, acclaim and enthusiasm for the publication of these daily zines. You see, a zine is an abbreviated version of a magazine. It seems to me that it would be an accurate description of you and Eydie as a specialized readership. Once in awhile the readership has been expanded, on a test basis, to determine the proclivity of others and so far they do not have any. But here is the definition of these daily publications. "A self-published paper, internet magazine, or other periodical, issued at irregular intervals with limited means (emphasis supplied) and usually appealing to a specialized readership." Does that nail it down, or what? The questions inserted at random here today do not require a response. They are in the nature of a rhetorical comment and you have told me with your body language that you do not want a pedantic explanation about such trivial matters.

However, having said all that which is supposed to have said nothing in keeping with previous issues, I will be more than glad to expand in whatever direction you think might be useless.

So as the great philosopher is said to have said you might want to look it up.

Dy

01/15/2001

## don belk young

From:        "don belk young" <donbelk@bellsouth.net>
To:          "john downey" <jjones2742@aol.com>
Sent:        Tuesday, January 16, 2001 9:09 PM
Subject:     INSPIRATION

The subject line is either a lie or a misnomer, but I did not want to be negative because I have not had much practice and am not very good at it. But the fact is that by the time I finally had a chance to sit down at the keyboard for the first time today, had just about run out of gas. However, there seems to be a dim light at the end of something out there that looks like a tunnel—is that not where you are supposed to see the light. Sure hope so. But then there was that other thing about the light being on the front end of the engine pulling the train at about a hundred miles an hour. Was able to use the entire day doing some golf, the annual meeting of the Credit Union members, a trip to FoodWorld (the highlight of the day), grilling some chicken. All in all, another exciting, fun filled day at the Young household.

Not long ago we had either an eclipse of the moon or the sun. It does not really matter which one. The point is that an occasion like that means that we have experienced a syzygy, a straight line connection of three celestial bodies. My source did not include any information about what a straight line connection of three human bodies Is called, but I think we could figure it out by just imagining a scene like that. Call it anything you want as long as it hard to spell and impossible to pronounce.

We expect to become well known, maybe even acquire some notoriety, when what we did yesterday becomes widely known. I know that we could rely on you for complete confidentiality but we must follow the rule of law and the will of the people and be sure that we avoid any possible confrontation about hanging chads or whatever it was that caused two or three people to behave rather badly during that syzygy. Actually that is what a disputed election was called until some folks in the Webster/Encarta cartel used it for something else. And they sure did not ask me. Have gone astray a little here, What we did yesterday, about 4 p.m. on Monday, January 15, 2001, will become widely known soon and we will give you a head start when we are able to do so.

The exit music is becoming audible and the lights grow dim. Must not be a train after all. Whew!!dy

01/16/2001

## don belk young

| | |
|---|---|
| **From:** | "don belk young" <donbelk@bellsouth.net> |
| **To:** | "john downey" <jjones2742@aol.com> |
| **Sent:** | Wednesday, January 17, 2001 12:18 PM |
| **Subject:** | QUIBBLES |

First, you must accept the rule that you cannot quibble about a foible. But then if you do not have a foible, then there is nothing to quibble about. Now is there. The upshot of quibbling when you do not need to and have been publicly ridiculed when you did is that you will reap the harvest of your errors, i.e., you will suffer the consequences of being inconsequential. Is there anything more fearful than demeaning. Well, yes there is. What if you were a zebu or were to become a plantigardi. All I can say about that is that if you were you would wish you were not.

So on to other less important things. We are having another exciting day. Went to the mailbox and found a leftover from yesterday's mail Had a temporary lapse (it wasn't a relapse because had not had it before) and suffered an attack of SLMS (Sloppy Mail Retrieval Syndrome). The only excuse I could think of was that it was dark when the mail was picked up and the usually deft digits known as fingers were not functioning as they have been trained to do. Anyhow, the item in the mailbox left over from yesterday was a Chrysler. So you can see that we had some excitement. But before that a real crisis had reared its head (not exactly ugly) and had to deal with non-delivery of the morning newspaper. Upon inquiry found that it was because I had been almost killed by a gunman who took my billfold with credit cards, etc., and the subscription renewal was supposed to be charged to my Discover so I could get that coveted refund each August. However, the renewal could not be put into effect until tomorrow so, of course, had to go to FoodWorld and get a newspaper. Tell me, what else could one do.

My gracious. Now comes the good part. As a reward for my perseverance and brilliant resolution of each problem that occurred so far today, I was permitted to prepare some cinnamon rolls. And so far that has been the highlight of the day except for a half dozen or so other things.

UAB has the awesome task of being the visiting team at Cincinnati tonight. Plan to listen to Gary but have some what do you call them trepidations.

Now for the rest of the day. If we are equally successful with the last half of the day as the first half, will have several more exciting experiences and they will be the meat and potatoes of future tines. On the subject of evidence which you inquired about, let's see, I think it was about 1982, have finally found a couple of descriptive terms. I would take credit for their creation, but they can be looked up in many reference books, so will just say That I could have thought of them if I wanted to. First Facts are stubborn things. Second: Some circumstantial evidence is very strong, as when you find a trout in the milk.

And on that lofty note, we find a stopping place so will rest for a couple of minutes.

You probably do not know that Lewisboro, New York is the location of the Waccabuc Country Club.

01/17/2001

**don belk young**

| | |
|---|---|
| **From:** | "don belk young" <donbelk@bellsouth.net> |
| **To:** | "john downey" <jjones2742@aol.com> |
| **Sent:** | Thursday, January 15, 2001 4:52 PM |
| **Subject:** | A SILENT EPIDEMIC |

It is a great temptation to send a blank page with a title of A Silent Epidemic. But my nimbus fingers could not resist when in place and a blank page confronted the LGC. You surely have jumped to a conclusion—that is the best way to get there, otherwise it requires thought, analysis and constructive conversation with those more learned—that my fingers are not nimbus. But you must be careful about a rush to judgment. Surely you know, as all scholars from John Wooden to John Gooden do, that you do not rush to judgment or jump to a conclusion, although that is about all the exercise some of us manage to work into our deify routine. No, no, nimbus is correct and proper as used. It does take a leap of faith, another exercise. You see, nimbus denotes an aura of splendor surrounding somebody or something. And I see no reason why that could not include fingers and brains. So the temptation to send nothing has been overcome by not permitting the frenum to deny freedom of movement of the fingers.

Frenum. You probably need a hint or two about that so that you will fully understand the first paragraph. It just would not be fair for you to not know as much about it as the rest of us. A frenum is a small fold of skin that limits movement of an organ. Now you are thinking that you have experienced firsthand, and probably on the other hand, too, a limitation of this type. Happily, it occurs among women mostly and it is a good thing. The frenum used most often is the one that connects the tongue to the floor of the mouth. Just think what would happen if female frenums were to become unrestricted in their range and flexibility. Should that occur, it would be an excess or overabundance known as nimiety and we would probably have 100 female senators making the laws of the land because they would have complete control of any filibuster. In my opinion this would not be a good thing but I have been wrong several thousand times so will not make any objections at this time, all the while resenting the right to have you do it for me whenever you would like to.

UAB beat Cincinnati 74-87 last night if you delete the first five minutes of the game. Yep, that's right. They have been losing by not scoring in the second half, but had an exceptional second half last night, but as the sage said, it was too small and not enough besides being inadequate. Cincinnati scored 14 points while UAB had zero in the first five minutes.

A rainy day in Harpersville today. Was at Oak City store until midafternoon. Accomplished very little and had an excellent opportunity to be depressed with rain, fog, and generally dreary impact on my bucolic lifestyle. May go by Edna's for a little cheer and nonsense. Edna readily admits that she jumped off the turnip truck. She said it was hard to make a comeback when she hadn't been anywhere, and that she started off with nothing and still has most of it. Have probably missed the free popcorn; must be there by 5:30 or so.

Unless you can find something following this sentence, that is all there is…
……………….dy

01/18/2001

**don belk young**

From:          "don belk young" <donbelk@bellsouth.net>
To:            "john downey" <jjones2742@aol.com>
Sent:          Friday, January 19, 2001 11:55 AM
Subject:       THE JONES FILE

Congratulations. You have achieved special status. The Jones File now has its own place on the desktop. It has been designated as such with the name "The Jones File" to distinguish it from the other two files which have not yet been named because they do not have a name or anything in them, i.e. devoid of content One of my critics—I have enough for both of us—has suggested in strong terms that determination of content is the province of the critic, not the creator. Since I did not have anything to say about that, I did not say anything because of the concern involving trepidation. Surely you have heard more than one orator say "It is not without trepidation...." when the speaker wanted to have a means of escape should the oration go awry. What the speaker meant was that it was with trepidation. As you know, he who hesitates to trepidate will hallucinate at large (at almost anybody). He might trepidate at a large antelope (opaid) or a large cantaloupe (mushmelon). It should be clear by now that what the world needs is a brouhaha instead of engaging in endless hypocritical broughtupsy (good manners) because their posole (thick Mexican soup) was served in a paper throwaway bowl. I think I need some help in getting out of here, but hesitate to ask. The last time I tried to help resulted in extreme embarrassment for both of us. Without revealing the unseemly details, let it be said that the face slapping was justified.

Congratulations to Miss Eydie. The editorial style is commendable. And about forgetting the paragraph with the clever riposte. It is quite an ordinary occurrence and a convenient way to disguise the gift of éclat so that you will not create expectations that you cannot possibly achieve on a consistent basis, especially when you try to accomplish such achievements on consecutive days.

John, you have probably earned a couple more Attaboys. As you know, you are the only honoree that has ever been granted a matched set of Attaboys. Actually, these were the only two ever conferred on anyone. The other 498 are around here somewhere. So you can see that you are either something special or no one else wants anything to do with such silliness.

Mr. Ray Boothe phoned this morning to report the good news and the bad news. The good news is that Jan is scheduled to go home tomorrow from Spain Rehab; the bad news is that she will have to put up with Ray's cooking. That is the gospel according to Ray. Will try to find out more details about whether Jan can regain her ability to be agile, mobile and hostile. Or was that something to do with football players.

Excitement rages on. Yes, this day is very much like all the other exciting days and it is with great tenacity that we resist the tendency to think that it is just another dull, ho hum, whatever, We do floors, go to the mailbox, call the cat, clean the litterbox, look at the calendar to be sure what day it is, and, in general—you must forgive this—keep up with the Joneses. Wonder if anyone has thought of that expression as a way of commenting on the tendency of all of us to think that we might be at risk to be "too soon old, and too late smart." I must capture these witty comments into something called "quotes for all occasions" or some such handbook. Must do some research on expressions like "gone to pot," "busman's holiday," "buy a pig in a poke," "strike while the iron is hot," etc. It seems to me that all of us have done all of these, but would not consider it to be editorially responsible to say so without independent verification by at least one clairvoyant. Perhaps a new limerick or two will do but who can do just two, perhaps you Adieu.

dy
everyone is ENTITLED to a struggle

01/19/2001

**don belk young**

| | |
|---|---|
| **From:** | "don belk young" <donbelk@bellsouth.net> |
| **To:** | "john downey" <jjones2742@aol.com> |
| **Sent:** | Saturday, January 20, 2001 9:19 PM |
| **Subject:** | INCONSEQUENTIAL TRIVIA |

Do you not agree that it is about time for some consequential trivia, as distinguished from inconsequential. For example, blonde jokes. Seems to me that Eydie had some of these in her repertoire at one time. But like most of us she could never remember the one she wanted to when it seemed like the thing to do. Anyhow, here is a list of the top 10 blonde inventions. I am sure that this is copied from somewhere but since I do not know the source, it will not be possible to expose their insentiveness, especially to those of us who are not blondes. We never get any good attention and it is not fair. Actually, it seems to me that we who are not blondes have been victimized.

Top 10 Blonde Inventions:

1. Water-proof towel

2. Solar powered flashlight

3. Submarine screen door

4. A book on how to read

5. Inflatable dart board

6. A dictionary index

7. Ejector seat on a helicopter

8. Powdered water

9. Pedal-powered wheel chair

10. Water-proof tea bag

Probably of much more interest and assuredly more useful is that a golf ball has 432 dimples. The thing is, that golf ball dimples are like snowflakes; no two are alike. I do not believe either of those prepositions.

Have you suffered MEGO lately. It seems to be occurring more and more frequently as the world spins around and so many things that occur have happened before which means that they are not unique or amusing or anything else so you get bored and your eyes glaze over.

Had another first today. For the first time in memory, which means that it could have happened any time before now, I went to the grocery store and got only those things that I was supposed to get when I first left the house. One loaf of raisin bread and two cans of Eagle brand condensed milk. You will recall that these are ingredients in the bread pudding. And so we have enjoyed some of that just now.

This mailing system has something called a spellchecker. Of course I do not need it because my spelling, like both of my other attributes, is impeachable. And it is an effective technique to stabilize the tendency to become arrogant, so we let it run at random and intentionally misspell certain key words like Eydie. The system keeps insisting that it must be Eddie. And in a recent note, must have been yesterday, we had a long battle about how to spell muskmelon. The spelling thing kept insisting that it was muskmelon, but I knew better and after much discussion and spirited debate, it was finally resolved in favor of the preferred spelling of every Illinois farmer that ever uttered the word. None of them know how to spell it but they sure know how to say it and, just like Wochjkzwoitz, it is spelled just like it sounds.

UAB just won their Tulane game at Tulane. Tulane is the team with nine players, five of them are freshmen. Next three games at home. Need to get it going.

The weekend is almost over and we weren't sure that it had started. Actually we started last Thursday and it has been so long that it should be over by now. So......bye...........dy

01/20/2001

**don belk young**

| | |
|---|---|
| **From:** | "don belk young" <donbelk@bellsouth.net> |
| **To:** | "john downey" <jjones2742@aol.com> |
| **Sent:** | Sunday, January 21, 2001 10:20 AM |
| **Subject:** | -ESQUE |

Today we will use a literary device. The only problem is that we do not know what it is. The technique is suffixal in nature, i.e., use of a suffix to more fully describe and give meaning to what would otherwise be just another trivial or inconsequential piece of junk mail. In case you missed it, one of the objectives of these messages is to get you out of the darkling syndrome. And another objective is to.....let's see, what was it. Anyhow, back to ESQUE.

Surely you, as a genuine, certified scholar, are familiar with the use of terms such as Reaganesque to describe a style of management, especially in politics and milking cows. The difficulty we (editorial we means me) have with this style is that such terms as Jonesesque and Youngesque and Eisenhoweresque do not trip off the tongue. They do not even fall off, just sort of cling there and cause gagging and other disgusting sounds. Besides, the use of such a technique has all the earmarks (can you have eyemarks or nosemarks) of trying to be noticed out of context. If you must be noticed, it should always be in context, don't you think? Another shortcoming (you never did enlighten us about whether one could have a longcoming) is the use of both long and short answers when a middle sized comment while standing In the middle of the road would suffice. This is leading to something called eponymous.

01/21/2001

## don belk young

| | |
|---|---|
| **From:** | "don belk young" <donbelk@bellsouth.net> |
| **To:** | "john downey" <jjones2742@aol.com> |
| **Sent:** | Sunday, January 21, 2001 2:25 PM |
| **Subject:** | -ESQUE II |

With no further explanation, will pick up where we stopped. Apparently this system continues to try to thwart and outsmart, notice the alliteration, my best efforts. When we left for our annual outing, I suggested, actually commanded the email file to place what will now have to be called -ESQUE I in the classification called "draft." You and I know what means. it is not yet finished and is not to be distributed. That is where my judgment was overruled and only when the culprit has been brought to justice will we relax our vigilance. Everything else is so relaxed that it is about to fall apart.

So where were we. Eponymous—to give a name to something. You can only do that if it does not already have a name, or you have been given unconditional authority to do whatever you want to. Or perhaps, in the manner of a select few of us, you can assume whatever authority you need that will fit the occasion. If I had any authority I would gladly delegate it to you, unconditionally and with malice aforethought and afterthought.

Occasional mention has been given to the thoughtfulness that goes into the preparation of these daily email messages. Since it will go without saying unless someone says it, I will say right now that any thoughtfulness that might find its way here has done so in an underhanded way and was not intended so do not be offended. One or two confessions may be in order but do not expect any from here except by accident. Words that are omitted or misspelled have been carefully selected. For example, in INCONSE-QUENTIAL TRIVIA, the last word in the first paragraph is prepositions. This was a test to determine whether you could tell that the real meaning was propositions. Or, more likely, you read it the way it was intended, as propositions and were not even aware of the presence of an o where an e should have been. In any event, I still do believe that no two snowflakes are alike, or that no two dimples in a golf ball are alike. Why? Because it defies logic and the law of gravity. The law of gravity is when you first realize that something is important. Grave, indeed.

We have now returned from a trip to AVCC where we successfully annihilated any lingering traces of anorexia. We knew we had succeeded in this noble quest when the blueberry cobbler and the key lime pie disappeared. So we are now sated, at least until supper time.

Editorial note: We are going to experiment with ClipArt, so you may receive something with no explanation at all. Might be quite refreshing when viewed in the darkness of all previous explanations. Don't know about you, but I find them personally rather sophomoric which is exactly what they are supposed to be. Would not want to rise above the horizon so far as to mistaken for sensibility or sensitivity.

Never look back. That fork in the road is probably no longer there. Bonjour, ami..............dy

dy
everyone is ENTITLED to a struggle

01/21/2001

## don belk young

| | |
|---|---|
| **From:** | "don belk young" <donbelk@bellsouth.net> |
| **To:** | "john downey" <jjones2742@aol.com> |
| **Sent:** | Monday, January 22, 2001 11:26 AM |
| **Subject:** | MAYBE LATER |

Right now is not a good time to be doing what I am doing because, contrary to what you may have been led to believe, sometimes there is a dearth of material, especially when the LGC are malfunctioning, which is becoming quite common. So we will carry on in the customary way and place one word after another until something brilliant or occult happens. I have no idea how occult got into that sentence. It obviously does not belong there. However we have become accustomed to first one filing and then two or three more irrelevancies jumping up and down if they are not included.

The weekend did go away at midnight. We did not pay any attention to it, having gone to sleep in between trips to the outhouse. Time-out! A tow truck just stopped in front of the house. OK. We took a thirty second time-out and decided to use a box and one defense to protect our property. And sure enough. They picked up the car of Jason's fiancée. You are not supposed to know who these people are and I will never tell because they have requested anonymity and as long as I have any I am willing to share. Share and share alike is what I always say as long as I get my share.

Do you think ODE TO A DIODE would be a suitable subject for a future dissertation. It has a certain lilt, although those D sounds need to be softened, don't you think. Also, the tale of Tallahassee has never been fully explained, has it? We either need a new burst of enthusiasm for this subject or forget about it. You would think that the seemingly supreme command of whatever subject comes to mind would yield, at a minimum, some inane drivel to fill up the space. We must resist the temptation to write just any-thing that comes along as a space filler. I say this with full assurance that you will not confide these confidences until my publisher has given per-mission to do so. We would have our advance by now but it was pre-empted by a note saying that any promise for any advance was false and misleading besides being an outright lie carried out by a perpetrator and dissembler. Never will forget the first and only time that I was described as a dissembler. Now there is another possibility. **TO DISSEMBLE OR NOT TO DISSEMBLE, THAT IS THE QUESTION**. I think you told me that such utterances are also a soliloquy.

Now we come to the long awaited and no doubt the best part. The end.

dy
everyone is ENTITLED to a struggle

01/22/2001

**don belk young**

| | |
|---|---|
| **From:** | "don belk young" <donbelk@bellsouth.net> |
| **To:** | "john downey" <jjones2742@aol.com> |
| **Sent:** | Tuesday, January 23, 2001 4:42 PM |
| **Subject:** | REVELATIONS |

Revelations that have been revealed here are rare and arrive on a very irregular basis and at random besides just happening whenever they want to, seemingly.

A recent revelation was something like "the road to hell is paved." This one was sort of hazy, but since our vast vista of experience includes all kinds of roads, we were able to discern (figure out, as they say in Southern Illinois) that the road to hell is not paved. It is a dirt road and when it rains the mud is so deep that you get what is called mired up to the axles. We did further research and found that this so called revelation was akin to the one that says that when you come to a fork in the road, you should take it. We went even further and determined beyond the shadow of a doubt that the sage who engineered this entire farce was trying to make a point about saying things that you did not mean or were not serious about. He was never able to articulate his revelation and thus it never became relevant.

When the sage was pressed to the wall by his students, he allowed that what he was trying to say was that "The road to hell is paved with intentions." it was immediately brought to his attention that intentions needed a modifier. What kind of intentions? Good? Bad? Mediocre? He then admitted that he had not ever had to deal with a bunch of intuitive Aquarians and had lost his grasp about abstract concepts under the pressure of the moment. Since the sage—his real name is Satchel Paige but no one believes that to be a real name, so he cleverly reversed the sound and has become known as Pascal Sage, which sounds like a real name—was so undone by this series of events that he could not function as a sage should, he delegated the final decision to Don Young—not his real name either, but he did not like the sound of Yon Dung—and so in a flash of dullness the matter has been resolved.

So we have brought this matter to an end, perhaps satisfactory, perhaps not. But put it all together and you now have a meaningful statement "*The road to hell is paved with good intentions*."

Humphrey Bogart was born today. So was John Hancock. Seems fair to me.

Entitlements, privileges, and Tallahassee are all matters that need to be dealt with. Right now there is something else that must be done so these will have to wait.

Have we used hasta la vista. Consider it done.

dy
everyone is ENTITLED to a struggle

01/23/2001

## don belk young

| | |
|---|---|
| **From:** | "don belk young" <donbelk@bellsouth.net> |
| **To:** | "john downey" <jjones2742@aol.com> |
| **Sent:** | Wednesday, January 24, 2001 4:08 PM |
| **Subject:** | JUST A LITTLE BIT TOO MUCH |

Got your note about yo need for funds for Jesse's Unwed Mothers or I May Be Messing Around. And have placed an unspecified amount in a trust in a Swiss bank account and an address in Costa Rica. So that has been taken care of.

Today was tremendously exciting. Golf, of course had first priority. Roy Kirkpatrick was there and he is having a very hard time. Having additional aches and pains himself and Rebecca broke (shattered) her ankle bones sometime in December and has been almost an invalid since then. Will be at least two more weeks before she can even think about touching that foot to the floor. Our foursome came in second place and we won $17.50 each so that worked out OK. Just got home and have several notes from Woowoo. An experience with a couple of dentists that she will tell you about sometime if you really want to know. Then to Dr. Bradley for follow-up on emphysema and stuff like that. Just called and we will meet at Lovoy's before going to the UAB game with Charlotte.

John, I have discovered another word and it helps to explain why you are not ept—read inept—at the keyboard. To do this properly, you must be a certified netizen. Apparently you have not yet achieved this status. I think it becomes apparent in an epiphanic way when it occurs. It is simply a combination word to identify one as a citizen who skillfully uses the *internet* Next time you see one, just say hello and be natural. If you do this in a proper and meaningful way, do not try to fake sincerity, everything will fall in place and probably shatter the silence.

We will talk about you at the ballgame and sure do wish you were here. Have not had a decent dirty martini since the last time we were in your kitchen.

Oh, also had a call from a broker who said they had sent me a dividend check by mistake. Will not write out here what I told him, but he will do "further checking." And the…well, gotta go….Dy

01/29/2001

## don belk young

| | |
|---|---|
| **From:** | "don belk young" <donbelk@bellsouth.net> |
| **To:** | "john downey" <jjones2742@aol.com> |
| **Sent:** | Thursday, January 25, 2001 5:19 PM |
| **Subject:** | ONE MORE CLEEK |

For lo these many years, I have had a cleek and never was aware of it until now. Did my daily review of the Encarta file and was struck with curiosity about what a cleek was. Now I realize fully (apparently that is the only way to realize—you know, to partially realize just would not slice the Poupon) that you may know or may not know anything about a cleek and that you may never want to know. The one I have was acquired about 40 years ago in a most unusual way. Michael was driving a tractor—he was seven years old but had a permissive grandfather—mowing grass on the golf course at Hillsboro Country Club. He saw this cleek in some trees and picked it up. It was brought to the house in Kirkwood and did not do a thing for many, many years. Then it resurfaced when we moved to Alabama, but it was put away again in a dark closet somewhere. Much later it was rediscovered for the third or fourth time. One time it was taken to Lovoy's for an independent appraisal and it was determined that it was worth almost nothing. But there was this fascination about it. The fascination has gone away but the cleek is still here. Actually it is leaning against the wall on one side of the room in which this composition is being composed. (Bet you would just as leave have it composted.) Most people, especially those who speak argot and street talk use the phrase "just as soon" when it is appropriate to do so, but many years of looking at the rear end of two horses while plowing have convinced me that the proper expression is "just as leave." Besides, that is the way that my Mom and my Dad and my Uncle Cary and my Aunt Alice and my Grandmother Pella and Grandfather Jake said it, not to mention my first cousins who are too numerous to mention, said it so that it how it has always been around here. I have not been able to figure out where to put a paragraph in this, so will just forget about OOPS, almost forgot to let you know what a cleek is. **A CLEEK IS A HICKORY SHAFTED GOLF CLUB.** Probably need a paragraph here. Why don't you just get out a ruler to follow the lines and I won't have to bother with the niceties of literary construction. Waitangi Day will be on February 6 this year. And it will be in New Zealand. Wonder where Zealand is. We have had much experience using New as the first word for names of places. New York. New Amsterdam. New England. New Hampshire. These places without the New in front of them are somewhere else. But where is Zealand. If we ever find it, will let you know posthaste. Sandral Hulett has been selected to be head of Cooper Green Hospital, I would take the time and effort to tell you a little more about Alpheus W. Halliday, but we have been exiguous today, therefore are not fully equipped to do it properly. Exiguous, pronounced ig ziggyou ess is a condition of barely existing with scanty or meager supplies. We do have some leftover chili and will probably have a full recovery so you can look forward to enlightenment on Halliday, Tallahassee, and I believe there must one or two more. Oh, there is one more thing. Someone told me sometime that they had received short shrift. I did not want to show my ignorance by asking what it was. But have you ever had one. Or did they mean long shrift. Do shrifts come in sizes? What is the largest one? Is it in the Guinness book of records? Are they like John or Jane Doe or Anonymous? Lot of questions. No answers. Must not despair. You may have a better day tomorrow if I can recover from whatever this is—could it be malaise or is it just another case of exercising my right to be eccentric. I think so. And as I have said many      times      before,      I      am      unanimous      in that!!!!!!!!!!!!!!!!!!!!!!!!!!!!!!!!!!!!!!!!!!!!!!!!!!!..................dy

01/25/2001

DON YOUNG

## don belk young

| | |
|---|---|
| **From:** | "don belk young" <donbelk@bellsouth.net> |
| **To:** | "john downey" <jjones2742@aol.com> |
| **Sent:** | Friday, January 26, 2001 10:06 AM |
| **Subject:** | THE SECRET |

In an attempt to maintain my readership, we continuously review the process and the procedures by which these messages are originated. Many kudos and self-congratulation have been given to the LGC. This source has been challenged and, upon further review, it has been established that the LGC are fallible. Sad to say but that is the conclusion of a couple of readers who do not have a proper appreciation for a writer who can skillfully omit a word at a critical point or intentionally misspell a word or two.

But the real message, **the secret** is "keep it simple." This is a well-known dicta and has become so widely accepted that it has a well-known acronym—KISS, Keep It Simple Stupid. The Stupid part refers to the party of the first part, also known as the creator. Not the great creator, just a smug, self-satisfied egomaniac at the keyboard. But to conclude the Keep It Simple message. The meaning is:

> "Use plain clear language. You may think fancy words make
> you sound smart, but it's more important to make sure read-
> ers understand your meaning than it is to impress them with
> your vocabulary."

The real problem with this rule is that it is in direct conflict with the Buckley/Young theorem. We are unanimous, again, that sagacity should be the rule of the day and should govern all civilized conversation, as well as street talk, Midwestern country talk, and rap. Alter all, and try to stay with me on this, sagacity is wisdom or discernment, whichever one is handy at the time, and it usually comes with profound knowledge and understanding coupled with foresight and good judgment. Now tell me, with as much candor as you can muster, would you have a simple comment or one faced with sagacity, and maybe a shot or two of rum.

I was struck with curiosity recently. You may not object to being struck every now and then, but it was not very pleasant at the time, especially because the curiosity was about whether one of these theses would be as well read the second time as the first. Well, as one with your insight and sagacity might expect, some do and some don't.

In the near future you can look forward to a mini lecture on entitlements and privileges. The basic message is if you have an entitlement or a privilege you should not give it away. And even more important, do not anyone else appropriate it and give it away. It makes you look like you don't care.

And we have not forgotten the promise about the origination of Tallahassee. And, of course, Halliday.

dy
everyone is ENTITLED to a struggle


01/26/2001


DON YOUNG

## don belk young

| | |
|---|---|
| **From:** | "don belk young" <donbelk@bellsouth.net> |
| **To:** | "john downey" <jjones2742@aol.com> |
| **Sent:** | Saturday, January 27, 2001 3:22 PM |
| **Subject:** | SATURDAY STUMPER |

Thanks for the accolades. And the same to you, O eruditious one. Your acknowledgment is somewhat belated, however. My mother was aware of my outstanding skills and ability to master new subjects a long, long time ago. For everyone else, it has taken a long time to grasp. Several hundred of my acquaintances never did quite get the message. On more than five or six occasions I have been referred to as a charlatan and just assumed that was at least as good as being a dissembler. To dissemble was explained previously and surely it is not necessary to repeat.

Spent some time with Ray and Jan today. She is quite confined, i.e., not mobile at all. And the fall caused her to have double vision so she cannot read very well. Apparently they watch the weather channel on TV mostly. I was at the house for about an hour and that was the menu. Both Ray and Jan said that she was doing much better. Goes to therapy three times a week, and someone comes to the house once a week to help with exercise, etc. They are not going to be able to use their basketball tickets. We tried to get Terry Smith to go with us, but she said she was not ready just yet.

Waitonya Day. Now that is a masterpiece of genius proportions. As I recall, some of your other proportions are not so masterful. To be specific, you mentioned "bank walkers." Jim Warden was the bankwalker in my swimming in the creek bunch, and I am very much aware of the awesome proportions that is required to be a certified bankwalker. It took just one phone call to determine that you were a watcher, not a walker.

Ray said that he had a phone call from Wes Ault. Was had been somewhere in Florida, was talking with someone there, said something about Ray Boothe, and the man had been in the military with Ray. J think his name was Art Jones.

Were you a disc jockey when you were selling cars. Seems to me that you would need a second job to eke out an existence in the car business. We noticed that your last two initials are DJ, and that perhaps your real name was Justa Disc Jockey. We have always known that there is no such name as John Jones because God just does not make that many mistakes.

In the world of the Thesaurus, just use the search ability of your computer. Type Encarta in the blank space and click on Search. Then you can look for any word, or, if you want to be like me, which is understandable, just imagine something and call it a word. For example, you have had borborygmus. Do not deny it, because we have been there when you were doing it.

Hope you enjoy the UAB/Memphis game. That will mean that UAB capitalized on the home court advantage. My prediction is that UAB will win by one point on a three point shot by Batchelor at the end of the game.

So what is a SATURDAY STUMPER. It is the crossword puzzle for January 27, 2001. Unless you know African lemur, American marsupial, Eminent immunologist, and Guidonian note, this one is lost.

> Great fleas have little fleas upon their backs to bite 'em
> And little fleas have lesser fleas, and so ad infinitum
> And the great fleas themselves, in turn, have greater fleas to go on
> While these again have greater still, and greater still, and so on.

dy
everyone is ENTITLED to a struggle

01/29/2001

## don belk young

**From:** "don belk young" <donbelk@bellsouth.net>
**To:** "john downey" <jjones2742@aol.com>
**Sent:** Sunday, January 28, 2001 12:00 PM
**Subject:** ADIEU, ADIOS, ARRIVEDERCE, AUF
WIEDERSEHEN, AU REVOIR, etc.

Your French lesson included in your note of Jan 27 is quite useful and instructive, especially the vous les vous item. It worked. I went to sleep right in the middle of it. You also indicated an improving grasp on imaginative use of words to mean whatever you want them to whether anyone else understands it or not. Indeed, you have grasped the true meaning of obfuscation, which means to clarify. To wit, short shrift becomes short shaft and then translates to short sheet. The French connection, and you surely are aware of the underlying meaning, is: "nappa pliee" is the French phrase for "folded sheet," and my advice is that if you get a positive response to "vous les vous couchez avec moi," you had better get that "nappa fliee" unfolded while she is taking her shoes off. All of this is a way of congratulating you on being endowed with both appetence and apperception, i.e., the desire or longing for something (appetence) and comprehension using past experiences (apperception). Neither of these endowments has anything to do with those usually associated with "bankwalkers." But then again, it might. And we do hope that you have not suffered unduly from borborygmus as a direct result of reading this paragraph to see the humor. Borborygmus is pronounced just like it looks, and describes "those rumbling sounds made by the movement of gases in the stomach."

You may have noticed, being one of the more alert readers, that there is more than one of saying goodbye. So the closing today is my learned attempt—the LGC are severely depleted—to provide the ultimate expression of a friendly farewell. Any question you have should be referred to a higher authority if you can find one.

**Word History**: More than one reader has no doubt wondered exactly how *good-bye* is derived from the phrase "God be with you." To understand this, it is helpful to see earlier forms of the expression, such as *God be wy you, b'w'y, godbwye, god buy ye,* and *good-b'wy*. It is no mistake to think that the first word of the expression is now *good* and not *God*, for good replaced *God* by analogy with such expressions as *good day*, perhaps after people no longer had a clear idea of the original sense of the expression. A letter of 1573 written by Gabriel Harvey contains the first recorded use of *good-bye*: "To requite your gallonde [gallon] of *godbwyes*, I regive you a pottle of howdyes," recalling another contraction that is still used.

And as anonymous said "A friend is one who dislikes the same people that you dislike."

dy
everyone is ENTITLED to a struggle

01/28/2001

DON YOUNG

## don belk young

| From: | "don belk young" <donbelk@bellsouth.net> |
|---|---|
| To: | "john downey" <jjones2742@aol.com> |
| Sent: | Monday, January 29, 2001 12;15 PM |
| Subject: | THE JONES FILE |

You have now earned shelf space. A file labeled "The Jones File" has been placed in a prominent place, between accolades to myself. Thought it would make you feel important. One of the accolades is a letter from John Gallalee, President of UofA in 1950, to Mr. and Mrs. Frank Young telling them that I was the best thing that happened to UofA since Ehney Camp. The other accolade is an unsigned Attaboy certificate with a blank place to fill in a name it a deserving person can be located. Has been a long, greeting search and no one qualifies.

Got your note about Eydie's blood counts and the UAB ballgame. Eydie, you got 124 words and the Blazers "went down like a one egg puddin." A one egg pudding is what you sent to John on the first day of Xmas. See email of January 5 for the compete rendition of the Twelve days of Christmas. You will be glad you did. In the process of the research to find the email regarding Twelve Days, I reread some of the earlier daily messages and was quite impressed. Some of them are so outstanding that when we take our biennial vacation trip, these will be reissued by my editor.

I am about ready to have a revelation. It is one of those things that may go in any direction and one must be alert or you will be bypassed. Or, more likely, it will diminish and be a minor revelation which is much less thrilling than the other kind. It could quite possibly cause cataplexy, a sudden temporary inability to move caused by ecstasy. This condition can occur at any time and usually without warning. I went to a charivari in 1938 (Owen and Kathryn Young) and had one. Awesome.

Lots of excitement in store today. Have already had our monthly from Rick. He counts ants, cockroaches, etc. and sprays accordingly. The cost for this $1.00 per ant, not to exceed 27 ants. So when several million of those critters—the Argentines are the worst—arrive, you save several million $ due to the $27 cap. Another exciting development was the telephone call to the dermatologist. Only had to wait four minutes and fourteen seconds, a new record. Have made six phone calls today and have not had to talk to a person yet. Probably a good thing because my ankles are sore, I need a shower, and cannot get to the concourse, so despite these exciting developments the expectations are that the pest control visit will be the highlight of the day. Maybe I will go to the library and search for something.

Tallahassee is about half way between Pensacola and Jacksonville. You must keep this in mind when the discussion about the location of Tallahassee is revealed. Note of warning. If this is not revealed to me, of course, it will not be revealed to anyone else. I was looking for revelations, visions, prophecy and future and found toasts, and here is one that will do until another comes along: "Here's to you, as good as you are,

> And here's to me, as bad as I am,
> But as good as you are, and as bad as I am
> I am as good as you are, as bad as I am."

Is that a good way to say goodbye for now, or what. Sure is.

dy
everyone is ENTITLED to a struggle

01/29/2001

DON YOUNG

## don belk young

| | |
|---|---|
| **From:** | "don belk young" <donbelk@bellsouth.net> |
| **To:** | "john downey" <jjones2742@aol.com> |
| **Sent:** | Tuesday, January 30, 2001 9:57 AM |
| **Subject:** | LESSER OF TWO WHAT |

"Whenever I'm caught between two evils, I take the one I've never tried."

You must know the source of the above quotation. I do, too, but my agreement to keep it confidential will remain in effect until a suitable arrangement for trying that new evil, whatever it is, can be arranged. With this introduction, it is obvious that there has been no improvement in the general quality nor any improvement in the tone and character of the message or the messenger. And say it always be. The secret is to drink some kumiss when you have this awareness that you are about to begin making sense and run the risk of becoming ordinary, average, everyday, normal, run of the mill, mine run, routine, bland, dull, unnoticeable, invisible to the naked eye, etc.

Excitement reigns. You may have noticed that when this is proclaimed that it does not happen. But that is very much in keeping with the tendency of almost everyone, not just politicians although they have perfected the technique, to exaggerate achievements and take credit for accomplishments of others. You should try it sometime. But about excitement. First thing that happened today was that nothing happened, at least nothing that was not supposed to happen. The garbage was picked up on schedule, the newspaper was delivered, the coffee percolated, the cat went outside, and the sun came up. The sum of these experiences cannot be overstated. Just think how exciting things would be if the sun did not come up. My bet is that we would not be thinking too much about the garbage and the coffee. About the sun coming up. That never happens. Galileo got put in jail for proclaiming that the earth came up, not the sun. As you know, and I know that you know because you confided at one time that you had some perceptions that had not been perceived by anyone else except Galileo. But the reality is that the earth is a planet rotating around the sun, so it is the earth that comes around the sun and therefore "comes up" each day. If you lived on the sun you would know for sure.

I do not know how we are going to get out of this today. Will now refer to my reference book which contains five thousand quotations, most of them trite truisms and quite useless, but occasionally one with a redeeming feature like it is one that I had never seen or heard of before, not even in a limerick. Hey, there is a thought. Let's end with a new limerick: "This **YOUNG** lad known as O'Toole; was known to be a fools fool; he was heard quoting Keats; while squeezing millions of teats; and sitting on a three legged stool."

Hope to have a full recovery by the morrow.

dy
everyone is ENTITLED to a struggle

01/30/2001

## don belk young

| | |
|---|---|
| **From:** | "don belk young" <donbelk@bellsouth.net> |
| **To:** | "john downey" <jjones2742@aol.com> |
| **Sent:** | Wednesday, January 31, 2001 3:35 PM |
| **Subject:** | TITILLATION |

Subject material for these dissertations are usually just some whimsical happenstance with no significance at all. And this is not a follow-up on yesterday's close with a mention of teat squeezings. That was thoroughly discussed previously and does not need to ever be mentioned again. But you seemed to be titillated with your mention of Halliday on January 28.

About Halliday. He was a selfish man in his way of living, and had no talent for gifts or giving. You probably do not recall the report about Halliday giving himself a present. It was little Miss Forbush out of accounting and she very sensibly turned to barley sugar.

> Stiffly but hungrily Halliday rose, picked up Miss Forbush and sampled her toes,
>
> Here was the answer to all his vague wishes, Little Miss Forbush was simply delicious,
>
> Anxious to linger yet hot to devour, he ate his way onward hour after hour,
>
> Just as he finished her brow and her hair, Old Mr. Halliday died in his chair,
>
> Too much free sugar and time that's been spended. Halliday's life was most tranquilly ended,
>
> Perfect his passing as sweet was his tooth, he died from an overindulgence in youth.

There is more, much more, to this Halliday thing but this.is probably all you need at this time. More likely, it is like the monkey and the skunk situation.

UAB is scheduled to try to play basketball this evening. We will be there. Should anything important at all happen while this is happening, you will be duly informed when it Is convenient to do so. Whatever is of superior quality, is of the highest standard, is genuine or authentic and properly done, will get its share of attention and will be forwarded to you promptly unless there is a good reason to withhold such tidings until you are better prepared. We know that you are puissant, but have serious reservations about your capacity for kumiss.

You may be offended by continued references to your inability to comprehend most of the literate passages that you are subjected to herein. There is a reason for this which will be revealed to you at an appropriate time. However, in the meantime, it might provide solace if you would keep in mind that "it is a mark of a superior mind to disagree and yet be friendly."

Sometimes it is necessary to use items just to fill up some space, especially when you have space that is unfilled and there is nothing else that will work. Here is one that we learned from you and our fondest wish is that it does not make any difference that you had forgotten it until it was mentioned here.

God grant me the senility to forget the people I never liked anyway, the good fortune to run into the ones that I do like, and the eyesight to tell the difference.

Remember, you heard it here first.

dy
everyone is ENTITLED to a struggle

01/31/2001

## don belk young

| | |
|---|---|
| **From:** | "don belk young" <donbelk@bellsouth.net> |
| **To:** | "john downey" <jjones2742@aol.com> |
| **Sent:** | Thursday, February 01, 2001 5:02 PM |
| **Subject:** | NOW I KNOW IT |

The book of quotations has become almost sterile because almost every-thing in it is something that you have enlightened many of us about on several occasions. You may know that, ask Eydie if you need to be re-minded, that you have a charming tendency to retell stories, but usually are able to make them enough different than the last time that the lis-tener is not quite sure where she has heard this one before. You need to be equipped with a dongle. Probably thought you already had one. However, there is a version in use now with computers whereby the de-vice called a dongle will, when plugged in, cause a program to be dis-abled. That should clear up whatever worries you have that you did not know what the hell you were doing trying to make that computer do something that it did not want to do. That is what a dongle device does for a computer. So, to bring this all the way around, you must have a dongle, probably under the control of a fairy or an elf or an angel or a gremlin or one of those little guys that hang around Irishmen.....any-how, it seems to work sort of like a birth control device. It keeps things from happening that otherwise would be just an ordinary, everyday kind of thing.

We hardly have ordinary things here because when we see one or experi-ence something that is supposed to be one, we call it something else. That is how we maintain a level of excitement that is at a higher decibel than your day to day monotone.

Went to Oak City Furniture today. It is somewhere between Chelsea and

Harpersville, and near Westover, Childersburg, Sylacauga, and numerous trailer parks of variable quality. Michael has a broken bone in his right arm and is practically disabled. He had, nevertheless, driven to Decatur for some furniture. Meantime, things were sort of busy at the store so have been back at the house for a short time and get around to reading today's newspaper and work the crossword, otherwise the day just might try to be more serious and dark and gloomy than it has a right to be. I would do another limerick or two, but a task of that magnitude is quite taxing and my golfer's nipple has been unusually tender today. About can tell you about that is that it in medical parlance, it is like tennis elbow, rower's rump, and dart thrower's wrist. It may help you to know that a right handed golfer tends to have golfers nipple on the left side of his chest from cloth abrasions. If you really need to know more about this, let me know in advance so we can think of an excuse to avoid any further discussion.

John, I have given a little, very little, thought to the idea that these diversionary messages might somehow become more widely read. Dave Barry's publisher has made some overtures but so far I have been able to ignore this source because they would not return my calls. One call that I did get, from one who insisted on being called anonymous, said that I should be given the cucking stool treatment. This required some research which would have been better forgotten. King Arthur was a second cousin to Odin; Odin is a god who is an ancestor of mine whose lineage can be traced to just about everybody. Arthur was known for several things, one of which was wide use of the tucking stool treatment for recalcitrant knights and anyone else who, in his sole determination, was deserving of such treatment. And woe to those to whom it was administered for it consisted to being tied to a stool, sometimes a commode (before running water), and pelted with rotting food.

I have so much fun doing these things, and almost everything else that comes along, that I have derived a couplet that might be considered for an epitaph, "Life is a joke and all things show it I thought so once, but now I know it!"

How's that for a final goodbye.

dy
everyone is ENTITLED to a struggle

02/01/2001

**don belk young**

---

| | |
|---|---|
| **From:** | "don belk young" <donbelk@bellsouth.net> |
| **To:** | "john downey" <jjones2742@aol.com> |
| **Sent:** | Friday, February 02, 2001 10:24 AM |
| **Subject:** | FOR JUST $8.99 |

One of the most significant developments in recent history occurred recently, but apparently has gone largely unnoticed. So it seems appropriate to avoid annoyance and resentment from some offense that most likely was intentional—that would be taking umbrage and we do not really need any of that. Umbrage is one of those words that sound ugly and contentious. And we must not judge too harshly in this season of mercy and forgiveness known as Groundhog Day in that place in Pennsylvania that has an unpronounceable name. No, no, that is not it at all. We are in danger of becoming extremely distracted here. Some would probably think of the incident I have in mind as having, perhaps, some local significance to a select few, but, at the same time, would not be construed by others as important except to perhaps three or four persons. But to set the stage. The venue for this scene is the local genuine, authentic Italian restaurant known as Villa Rosa. You know about this, having been one of the early patrons and participating lustily in devouring the pasta of the day known as lasagna. The management of Villa Rosa recognized the naturalness with which Woowoo and I dealt with the complications of deciding, ordering, and consuming the culinary delights. So it was arranged for a copywriter and a photographer to capture the scene of the two of us with Reyna and another lady enjoying an authentic Italian meal. Then it was duplicated on an 81/2 x 11 page and reproduced by the millions, more or less, and included with the other thousand pages or so of advertising that accompanies most of the newspapers delivered each day. The picture is worth at least a thousand words, and the caption across the bottom of the photo says that you can have lasagna, baked ziti, and a couple other entrees, including salad, fresh baked bread, etc. for JUST $8.99. Can you believe that. In the spotlight again. We have agreed to make celebrity appearances without expecting an appearance fee in exchange for having one of the muddled martinis labeled the Woowoo wobble. You may not be aware that Woowoo, unlike other one named celebrities like Cher and Madonna, has chosen to remain anonymous. You could say that she is unanimous in being anonymous. We do promise that, regardless of whatever fame comes this way, we will use it for noble purposes. Furthermore, we will continue to see both of our friends, although it may be necessary to do so by appointment only to maintain proper decorum and under no circumstances would we ever allow any umbrage to occur.

dy
everyone is ENTITLED to a struggle


02/02/2001

## don belk young

| | |
|---|---|
| **From:** | "don belk young" <donbelk@bellsouth.net> |
| **To:** | "john downey" <jjones2742@aol.com> |
| **Sent:** | Saturday, February 03, 2001 4:08 PM |
| **Subject:** | DU JOUR |

It is axiomatic, or should be, that anything du jour is better than something that is not. As you instructed me during one of those crucial discussions involving something, if you are inclined to soliquolize, it is better to do a soliloquy du jour than to do almost anything else. This du jour thing has become almost garrulous (excessive, talkative, wordy), don't you think. But there is a purpose. After a relatively calm morning today, the afternoon is teeming with excitement. Auburn and Ole Miss are trying to finish a nail-biter, UAB has just jumped to a 7-0 lead playing at Southern Miss, and, TA TA, best of all, the du jour of the day is vegetable. Soup, that is. Will be ready for first tasting about 4:30. If you did not want to know this, you can just skip the first paragraph.

Anonymous has been busy again. This just in from A. "A pessimist is one who feels bad when he feels good for fear he'll feel worse when he feels better."

It would be accurate to say that writer's block has suddenly developed. It could also be argued that the LGC have taken leave of their senses and gone off somewhere to recuperate. Probably best to just not do anything so that is the work du jour for right now. Will be back.

We are back. Have just finished pretending to meditate. This requires a total lack of concentration and an ability to use all that black space inside the cranium. Like most black places, it does not do anything, either. So when you are not doing anything it becomes relatively easy to think of yourself the way others do, and the way you tend to think of others, to wit, that you have, become useless or will soon reach that highly desirable status. Only in this way can you be consistent and not get blamed for doing this or that because you have not done anything. It is also known as a circumstance when you have fallen asleep unintentionally. Come to think of it, probably can't fall asleep intentionally even if you intended to do so. You would be thinking about your intentions and might get them mixed up between good and bad—intentions, that is. And it is not a good person who has bad intentions on purpose. How about an intention du jour. Might as well. But in all candor, this seems to have a new level of inanity. Unfortunately it is not likely that we will be able to maintain this status.

But will try once again soon. Let me know if you want a day off.

dy
everyone is ENTITLED to a struggle

02/04/2001

## don belk young

| | |
|---|---|
| **From:** | "don belk young" <donbelk@bellsouth.net> |
| **To:** | "john downey" <jjones2742@aol.com> |
| **Sent:** | Sunday, February 04, 2001 10:18 AM |
| **Subject:** | UNTITLED |

Please notice that the title of this one is UNTITLED. May have created an oxymoron by saying that the title of an untitled essay (3286) is untitled because then it becomes titled and is not entitled to a title because it is untitled. Should be obvious that the dry spell continues as far as brilliant, far reaching philosophical soliloquies are concerned. UAB won 70-59.

Your club number may appear anywhere in this newsletter. You have won something, but requires that you send cash by messenger in advance in cover handling charges. The amount will be determined when we have ascertained (found out) how much cash you have. If you say you have none or some other ridiculous amount, we will have a serious discussion of sources from which you can obtain same. The potential bonus is that you will be treated to as large a bowl of soup du jour as you can handle. But excessive slurping will cause disenfranchisement as far as seconds are concerned. We know you do not want that so mind your manners, not to mention your p's and q's.

P's and q's has potential for a future email when something like UNTITLED does not come to mind.

Speaking of Mind, do you get the UAB Reporter? We get one, usually two or three weeks later, and, quite frankly, seldom see anything of interest. A recent issue, however, features an experiment at UAB in which two faculty members have designed a course about the MIND/BRAIN. It seems that the mind and the brain are two different things. Sort of like body and soul.

Or a concept and a thing. So be careful when you refer to the LGC, and we will do the same. You may be confusing the mind and the brain within both the mind and the brain. What a concept Is this a great country, or what? I will be so bold as to answer that question. Although it is a rhetorical question and it is not polite to give answers to such, this writer has been known to give answers which did not have any kind of question. It's a matter of style. The answer to the question "Is this a great country, or what?" is that it is a what. Let me enlighten you about how this conclusion was concluded. We know it is a great country. We were told that in first grade (did not have kindergarten) and have never had a reason to question it, rhetorical or otherwise. So we know that Is true. Stay with me here. We are approaching this from the third side of a Pythagorean triangle. So we know that without saying that it is a great country. So why was the question asked if the answer is so evident. Aha! It is because it is really a what. Why else would the question be asked. In some circles a person who arrived at this conclusion in this way would be called a square even though it was being discussed in a circle. It is not always a just world. And that gives me a segue to a closing with this clever? saying. You have heard it before but now it is written for all to enjoy, including those who cannot remember a couplet, let alone a limerick.

"The rain it raineth on the just, and also on the unjust fella;
But mostly on the just, because the unjust stole the just's umbrella."

So on this Sabbath, let us conclude with a hallelujah !!!!!!!!!!!!!!!!!!!!!!!!!!!!!!!!....dy

dy
everyone is ENTITLED to a struggle

## don belk young

| | |
|---|---|
| **From:** | "don belk young" <donbelk@bellsouth.net> |
| **To:** | "john downey" <jjones2742@aol.com> |
| **Sent:** | Monday, February 05, 2001 11:26 AM |
| **Subject:** | "IF...AND ONLY...IF" |

Today we will discuss a logical constant. For example, the expression "if...and only...if," when used in formal logic, is a constant By way of deductive reasoning, which is employed here when we do not see an obvious conclusion, an informal constant or a formal inconstant, would not be a logical constant. But we digress again. is there a prescription for antidigressant. If, and only if, we could find one it would prevent these discretionary digressions which have become prevalent And there are a lot of them, too.

Your email arrived about noon yesterday but we were having one of those busy, exciting days and did not go to the email box until early Mon. a.m. There it was. The highlight of the day was an encore performance by the soup du jour of another du jour. The embodiment of the flavor, especially in the carrots, was cause for celebration, so we went to the library and did some research on rheumatoid arthritis. Actually, it was t'other way 'round. Woowoo is having an occasional attack of—we do not what to call it except what it looks like—blue fingers. Remember the song "Am I Blue." If you asked Woowoo, she would show all her fingers at the same time and let you figure it out for yourself. If you know what it is, she would appreciate it if you would share such information as you might have access to. How to make sense out of various symptoms is a genuine dilemma. Makes you want to get all the doctors in one room at the same time to try to get a systematic way to deal with which Rx does what, how they work with each other, etc.

We were glad to know that Eydie continues to improve and our wishes are that all things go in the right direction. When we can do anything you know that we will.

About a preface for the tome to be published with these daily chronicles. I am not sure that I could stand to be prefaced by Monica and that is all I am going to say about that. I do enjoy a good cigar. I really do. And l think it was demonstrated that, without question, you can have a preface and a cigar at the same time. There are occasions, of course, when you just have to bite the bullet and take a risk. As that great philosopher was famed for saying "The right to be a cussed fool, is safe from all devices human; it's common (ez a gin'l rule) to every critter born of woman." In this case it does not make any difference whether you have xenophobia or not.

So we conclude as we began with a logical constant....if, and only if...dy

dy
everyone is ENTITLED to a struggle

02/05/2001

**don belk young**

---

**From:** "don belk young" <donbelk@bellsouth.net>
**To:** "john downey" <jjones2742@aol.com>
**Sent:** Tuesday, February 06, 2001 10:20 AM
**Subject:** THE SECRET

Questions have been forthcoming about how one acquires a talent. Something in the Bible about that but it has not been revealed to me, probably because you must open the book and look in the index to find out where it is explained. But not to digress is the rule as was explained yesterday or if you do not recall or do not want to look for it in the index, just imagine how easy it is to digress and then do not do it. Matter of mental discipline and oral hygiene. If you keep your mind closed, your mouth shut, and your brain idle, no one will be able to determine whether you have any or not. Any what, you might be inclined to inquire. Any digressions, of course. THE SECRET is not a secret in a secretive sense because you cannot acquire it by secretion. There are two ways to acquire talent and it is not a secret in the literal sense of the general meaning. Hope you did not get lost there because we are going somewhere. Talent can be provided no sooner than conception and no later than forever. Most common way to get some, talent that is, is to work for it. Now you know. There are a case or two where talent has been granted posthumously. This occurs when the descendants make up stories, sometimes called outright lies, about the accomplishments of their ancestors white conveniently ignoring the defects of same. It requires much less mental and/or physical effort to obtain talents A.D., but it is not very satisfying. Makes you wonder why the relatives even do such Things. Tch, tch.

It does not seem fair for the writer to have any advantage over the reader(s?) so will provide you with some information that you do not really need but you might be offended or feel neglected if it was withheld. **1.** There is more than one logical constant, subject of yesterday's literary discussion, but we will have no further comment unless popular demand demands that we do. **2.** Waitangi Day is here. The New Zealanders would appreciate appropriate recognition. My personal preference is Cinco de Mayo. **3.** Today marks the Festival of Aphrodite. This is mentioned only because it occurred to me that someone might want to know. I actually saw Aphrodite, let's see, must have been about '38, maybe '39, it was before the war. Went to a circus in Litchfield and my brother lifted the flap of the circus tent to permit my illegal entrance to sea him/her.

Okay, class. Let us turn our attention to sentence construction. The project of the day is to include amok, clads, and trode in a sentence. The way they were worked into the previous sentence does not count So here is a shot at it. We trode amok the clarts.

Excitement reigns supreme again. Don't remember what we did yesterday, but already today we made a follow-up appointment with a dentist for three crowns, Horace came by for his tax returns, and we trode amok the darts.

That is all there is to it, so tally-ha.                                              dy
**dy**
**everyone is ENTITLED to a** struggle

02/06/2001

**don belk young**

From: "don belk young" <donbelk@bellsouth.net>
To: "john downey" <jjones2742@aol.com>
Sent: Wednesday, February 07, 2001 4:27 PM
Subject: MISSED OPPORTUNITIES

The burning question right now is in regard to missed opportunities. The central issue here is how do you know you have an opportunity that is about to be missed before it gets away. Say that an opportunity is right there waiting for anybody to do something with it and nothing happens. Perhaps those who missed it did not even know that it was there. They will be better off if they never find out that they missed it because if they do find out, the most likely upshot is that they will be disappointed. Even worse, their mothers will be even more disappointed and that is when things can get really complicated. Two disappointments in the same family at the same time could lead to despair and despondency and create a disturbance. Also be unsettling to both of them. But the real challenge is to know an opportunity when you see one. They have no defining characteristics that are apparent to the naked eye, and many times cannot be seen even when you are equipped with prescription spectacles. Therefore, may we suggest that you look back and recall the last opportunity that you missed and forgive yourself. Then take the one before that and forgive yourself. Keep on until you have nothing to regret. The "forgive yourself" advice is obvious when you think about it. The point is that no one else is going to give you carte blanche forgiveness so just go ahead.

Now that you feel better, go ahead and do it for both of your friends.

There are 293 ways to make change for a dollar. And if you have three quarters, four dimes, and four pennies, you have $1.19. You also have the largest amount of money in coins without being able to make change for a dollar.

Have searched my file for witticisms, humor, pithy sayings, and lore and wisdom, not to mention fustian utterances, but to no avail. Decided to make up some of these but it was too taxing and, like most everybody, we do not need any more taxes so gave up on that. I suppose all in all, you could say that it was just one more missed opportunity. Since we know how to deal with that, we will take this opportunity to sign off for now.

dy
everyone is ENTITLED to a struggle

02/07/2001

**don belk young**

| | |
|---|---|
| **From:** | "don belk young" <donbelk@bellsouth.net> |
| **To:** | "john downey" <jjones2742@aol.com> |
| **Sent:** | Thursday, February 08, 2001 1:54 PM |
| **Subject:** | ATTACHMENT |

THE ATTACHMENT IS NOT REALLY AN ATTACHMENT. IT IS A SEP-
ARATE DOCUMENT AND HAS BEEN DUPLICATED AND EMAILED
ALL BY ITSELF SO THAT YOU WILL NOT HAVE TO BE CONCERNED
ABOUT HOW TO OPEN AN ATTACHMENT TO AN EMAIL. I say this
so that you will know that I know that you do not know how to do that
except when it works, and even then you do not know why.

Have already been to Harpersville. It looks like this location will do OK
but it is a building process. Michael knows that he is starting over. He is a
typical entrepreneur—just because it did not work once does not mean that
you should not keep on keeping on.

The attachment is a copy of the public statement made by the Reverend
Jackson regarding recent events. It had been forwarded so much by the
time it came to my attention that it was necessary to retype. Just my way
of maintaining the high standards of these writings. Self-imposed discipline is the best kind. I have attempted to accept discipline from others but
it just did not work. Since it was obvious that I needed some, I decided to
do it to myself and now everyone can see that I am a much better person
than you used to be. Yes, there is hope for all.

The main source of excitement today is finding a couple of words with revealing characteristics. Dunno, for example, has been added to the list of
acceptable words and means just what you though it did—don't know. But
the jewel of the day is dunnakin. Oh, how wonderful it would have been

if we could have told our mother that we had to go to the dunnakin. That's right. It is an outside toilet. One good thing about a dunnakin is that you could clearly see the ballet of the bathroom when someone was inside with the door locked, and the ballet was being performed by one waiting outside in clear view of anyone who happened to be there. In our modern circumstances, the bathroom ballet usually occurs when the stalls are full, but is out of sight except for other members of the troupe. And not a tutu in sight. The contents of this paragraph are apodictic since they are indisputably true.

Will sign off now and go directly to the project to republish the Public Statement of the Rev. Jesse Jackson. Enjoy.

dy
everyone is ENTITLED to a struggle

02/09/2001

## don belk young

**From:**     "don belk young" <donbelk@bellsouth.net>
**To:**       "john downey" <jjones2742@aol.com>
**Sent:**     Friday, February 09, 2001 4:53 FM
**Subject:**  THE WEEKEND HAS STARTED

One more weekend of excitement may be more than a normal person should have to experience. It will be not a problem for one who is not normal because if you are not normal how do you know whether you are having a good time or not. All of those around you, and millions who are somewhere else, and billions who have never heard of you, may be having what they think is a good time but when you take a closer look, well, it may not be a big deal. Let us assume that we are normal and all those weird folks hanging around are normal also, at least as far as they are concerned. So what is all the excitement about. Maybe we can contrive a happening or two that would qualify.

But a couple of loose ends. It seems that a recent email may have been closed rather summarily with an incomplete explanation of certain terminology, namely, "we trode amok the clarts." If you were confused and thought it would be unbecoming to go to the trouble to find out what that was about, we will undertake to clear up any misinterpretation you may have made. Without meaning to take away the privilege of allowing you to let it mean any damn thing you wanted it to, feel free to make up your own dog story about it. You seek darts is/are those little clumps of mud that cling to your shoes and will just not let go. It is worse with so-called tennis shoes than almost any other kind so avoid these when you can and, whatever else you may be permitted to do as far as dressing yourself , never wear tennis shoes and a bow tie at the same time. Aargh! Back to the clarification. Amok is self-explanatory so the rest of it is quite routine, unless you are also remiss in the knowledge of tootle. But I cannot recall exactly what it is either so as was indicated above, just let it be whatever you want it to.

And the other loose end involves your clever transmission entitled "Redneck Medical Terms." The minute we saw the title we just knew that there was no such thing. And your transmittal served perfectly to confirm that conclusion. The body of the letter was a blank page. We were so pleased that you had not lost your sense of humor, just out of whack a little but in such a way that it had even more impact than a dry sponge. Reminded us of that expression about "some went to look for it and it wasn't even there, so they grabbed any old tail off any old hook."

UAB on TV at 1 p.m. tomorrow vs USE. Should be rested and ready to finish the season on a winning note. Only eight games to go; post season would have to be classified as unlikely right now.

My brother Frank called from Coffeen, Illinois, last night. They will stop here for supper with us Sat. night on their way to some place south of Orlando. He confirmed that they had a real winter this year. Snow still on the ground in Southern Illinois. You need to know more about Coffeen. I will give some consideration to a request to provide more information, but it would be a great deal of trouble and I will not use up my valuable time with such trivia for no reason at all. Coffeen does not have a Chamber of Commerce so it is not easy to find out what is going on there.

Who was it that said "Methinks thou doth protest too much"? More about that another time but for now that's it!

dy

02/09/2001

## don belk young

**From:**       "don belk young" <donbelk@bellsouth.net>
**To:**         "john downey" <jjones2742@aol.com>
**Sent:**       Saturday, February 10, 2001 9:19 AM
**Subject:**    AD HOC ABSURDUM AD NAUSEUM
                AD INFINITUM

The spirit of the day or week or month has been elusive during these try-ing times but we may have captured the general mood with the selection of the subject line for today. You would be surprised and impressed with the amount of thought and preparation, not to mention getting ready and lying awake probing for inspiration that also remains elusive most of the time. But today we have struck the mother lode. Surely you will agree that absurdum captures the essence of inanity. Hey, maybe that would be the title page for the soon to be published collection of "john downey" essays. The book would consist of placing on each page the title of the essay for that day and leaving the page blank. The reader would be chal-lenged to write her or his own version of the silliness of the day. ESSENCE OF INANITY! Yes, I think that might work. Did you ever find that feller that thought he could sell it on the corner in a paper sack? Nei-ther did I.

As usual we are faced with another exciting day. We do not know what it is going to be. The anticipation that something out of the ordinary will occur is always present. The odds of anything at all happening are about one to one, take your pick. Like most challenges this one will be met if it shows up. Should that not occur it will remain a mystery about what might have been. And you have my word on that.

I know how much you appreciate the historical footnotes from "The Rise and Fall of Almost Everybody." Here are a couple more from another source. I do not believe the source can be traced so will admit that they were thought up while having a sip of B&B a day or two ago.

1. In Scotland several hundred years ago, a new game was invented. It was entitled Gentlemen Only, Ladies Forbidden... and thus the word GOLF entered the English language.

2. In English pubs, ale is ordered by pints and quarts. So in old England, when customers got unruly, the bartender would yell at them to mind their pints and quarts and settle down. It's where the get the phrase "mind your p's and q's."

There are some more of these where one could get footloose in the footnotes of history, but you can only manage this Idiocy in small doses so will work them in from time to lime. Will need to be very careful with the one about getting consent of the King to have a baby. Really! And to titillate a little more—I think I did that to you a couple of times already so you should be inured—we have the inside info about the phrase "wet your whistle" and "goodnight, sleep tight."

dy
everyone is ENTITLED to a struggle

02/10/2001

**don belk young**

| | |
|---|---|
| **From:** | "don belk young" &lt;donbelk@bellsouth.net&gt; |
| **To:** | "john downey" &lt;jjones2742@aol.com&gt; |
| **Sent:** | Sunday, February 11, 2001 10:58 AM |
| **Subject:** | BUT |

We appreciate your thoughtful process toward understanding the wide variety of subjects undertaken here. But your admission that you had to read some sentences twice to understand them was completely unnerving. Many of these sentences have never been read by anyone but you. We do not look back and do not proofread lest we would be inclined to make changes that would distract from the senseless character that separates them from all other writings. But I digress. You are not supposed to understand most of this stuff. Next thing we know you will have us established as normal, and that sounds like average, and no one wants to be average, even those that are way, way below average. But let us continue. Have you noticed the use of "but" to start a sentence. Of course that is acceptable writing style. But it should not be overdone. You are free to disagree. But you should not do so.

So the plot today is to demonstrate the absence of the required number of genes to keep up with the Joneses or whoever else might seem to be better off. You know what a fruit fly is. Let us know if you need clarification on this A fruit fly has less than 15,000 genes. And you have about twice that many. Therefore, employing reasoning and deductive powers, you would be twice as genetic as one fruit fly or equivalent to two fruit flies, wouldn't you say. Furthermore, male genes are more likely to be deficient In some way than female genes. This information is based on research conducted by women and may be slanted just a little to keep the males from getting too cocky. Besides, it equips females with qualities and characteristics that lets them feel comfortable when the male gets time anxiety, usually notice-able by getting in the car and starting it while the female is trying to get her fingernails finalized. You must be able to deal with "Waitonya" in such a way that it is not detectable so that you do not get classified as an impa-tient oaf. JAP is the initials of a well-known UAB figure who strongly be-lieved that "punctuality is a waste of lime." His essay about punctuality is a classic.

JAP is? Since the initials are plural, this reference probably should have been JAP are. Use whichever one you think sounds right or looks OK. But do not bother to tell me which one is correct because it makes not a whit of difference.

A gigerati must exercise his digastic. And if he is a digamist he must be even more diligent to be certain that all two-part muscles are properly ex-ercised. If you understand that I have failed in my attempt to be uninfor-mative. My next projects is to attempt to write a humorous verse about a named person where the person's name is the first verse. This is known in literary circles as a clerihew.

Until the 'morrow. BUT you never know.

dy
everyone is ENTITLED to a struggle

02/11/2001

## don belk young

**From:** "don belk young" <donbelk@bellsouth.net>
**To:** "john downey" <jjones2742@aol.com>
**Sent:** Monday, February 12, 2001 9:48 AM
**Subject:** ABOUT BRIGHT WOMEN

Eydie, your email suggested that women are bright and gave one reason. You implied that there were many reasons but that you would restrain yourself by sending the very first one about the Titanic. As long as you are willing to be restrained, the best way is to do it to yourself. If someone else does it, you get your feelings hurt and we can't have any of that in our civilized environment. We have learned that feelings are more important than reality and there is no basis for any other conclusion. To be restrained is better than to be cullied. The last time I was cullied was in a poker game when John had all the answers in his shirt pocket. Self-restraint is a wonderful human trait that is provided to the more select The problem is that we do not know who gets to do the selecting. Self-selection might work but seems to be self-serving.

Probably the best way to deal with daily dilemmas, whether they are self-imposed or otherwise, is to exercise a prerogative every now and then. You could also be hegemonous, which is the same thing, more or less. The hegemony thing needs to be done with compassion, otherwise the one to whom it is being done will feel dominated and controlled and thus lose his/her self-esteem. The title of this one would be more appropriate if it were called SELF. Back to exercises. Jumping on the band wagon, leaping to conclusions, etc. are the only exercise available to many. So I would reiterate, say again, be sure to exercise your prerogative on a regular basis. On a personal note, mine has not been exercised in this millennium, so will take my own advice and go off somewhere for twenty or thirty minutes one of these days without requesting permission from anyone except myself. There goes that self word again.

Eydie, I would give you another reason "why women are so bright," but cannot think of one. These essay projects are usually prepared in the afternoon when my senses have been sufficiently dulled that the only thoughts that I can think of are not very thoughtful and as a result we get those that occur at random and seem to be the result of the ricochet phenomenon— bouncing around inside the cranium. When they get outside they become quite dangerous to your sanity by finding their way to this piece of paper through the fingertips and the keyboard.

Have this sudden affliction known as MEGO. So must go. MEGO and MUST GO are not related, so do not try to make any connection. Just relax and be sure to get your exercise.

dy
everyone is ENTITLED to a struggle

02/12/2001

## don belk young

**From:**         "don belk young" <donbelk@bellsouth.net>
**To:**            "john downey" <jjones2742@aol.com>
**Sent:**         Tuesday, February 13, 2001 1:18 PM
**Subject:**     I WISH I COULD

Do you agree that reading this line from left to right and then reading the next line from right to left would be much more efficient on the eyeballs. Once upon a time in an ancient place the focal scribes and more erudite amongst them devised this method of written communication. Apparently it was restricted to those who had been certified by the shamus or whatever they called their local witch doctor because those writings on the caves near Vincent, Alabama are not written in any understandable, systematic way. The horses look like they are running backwards in some instances but not in such a way that this type of written communication would qualify as boustrophedon, which is the descriptive word that Aristotle, Euphrates, Glaze, donbelk, and a few lesser intelligentsia in the Mensa group have used for to these many centuries to describe this type of writing. You can take my word for it. Or you can try one more time to look it up.

Dwelling on a subject is not a sign of good mental health. Since this type of affliction has not been a deterrent in the past, we will ignore such signals again. So to follow-up on the idea of boustrophedon as a more efferent way to read would you please let us have your thoughts along these lines. It just seems like the logical thing to do and it would help you, too, besides all the benefits. For instance, your eye tendons that make the lens and the iris and the cornea and all those other eye parts do what they do, would have less wear and tear. Perhaps this would solve the dilemma of those who do not even know that they have a dilemma or any other kind of problem. Preventative treatment we would call it. That means that you fix it before it breaks, a step ahead of "if it ain't broke, don't fix it."

The prophet Paige advised against looking back and we will not violate that advice except in a peripheral way. Instead of looking back, in a technical sense, all we have done here is to look up to the first paragraph and noticed a reference to Euphrates. And must confide to you that "it just don't look right." Without going into any extensive research on this matter—we find it convenient to ignore any conclusion that is "based on extensive research by an independent laboratory" because it might persuade one to reach a conclusion that one does not want to reach. With that explanation, I will reveal my innermost thought about Euphrates. I think he was a river, not a person. There is always the possibility that the river was named after the person, probably by himself, or that the person was named after the river, probably by his mama. For the sake of argument, let us put the matter to rest by taking a small nap.

So until wake up time.

dy
everyone is ENTITLED to a struggle


Footnote for the inconsequential trivia file.

> Pub patrons in merry olde England had individual ceramic cups. Many of them had a whistle baked into the handle. When a patron wanted a refill he would use the whistle. The phrase "wet your whistle" was inspired by this practice.

02/13/2001

## don belk young

| | |
|---|---|
| **From:** | "don belk young" <donbelk@bellsouth.net> |
| **To:** | "john downey" <jjones2742@aol.com> |
| **Sent:** | Wednesday, February 14, 2001 4:10 PM |
| **Subject:** | :-) :-) :-) |

:-) The symbol immediately preceding the word "the" in this sentence is a smiley face and it has a name, namely emoticon. A clever combination of emotion and icon put together by some computer nerds to try to explain some of their silliness. Why anyone would degrade themselves by participating in any sort of silliness is one of the things that I will never understand. The other two things that we have already agreed on that we do not understand are arbitrage and dames. That is almost as bad as bazoode. That is the stuff you get in the Caribbean and causes one to not be able to think clearly, as well as to be confused and dazed. It was not mentioned, even in an allegorical way in my reference source, but it is obvious that it is a contraction of bamboozled, which you must know means that you are drunk.

It is no accident that the writing style has been simplified so that you can get the meaning with a single reading. Meticulous. In a word that is the way to go when you want to be extremely careful and precise.

We are well into another exciting day. I have already won $13 at Attadena Valley Country Club. Woowoo is with Dr. Bradley. Still working out how to breathe easier. Got some free advice about who to see about the continuing tendinitis in the heel bones which are connected to the leg bones— well, we won't go through the anatomy lesson this time. UAB has a game with Marquette at 7 p.m. Must win is the name of this game. The cat is inside after being out most of the day. It is such a comfort to know that YumYum, that is the name of the cat, is safe and comfortable. The weather is unremarkable in a hazy, dreary sort of way.

And on that note of care and understanding will close for today. It would just not be right to close on a note of discord. I say that if you have a choice between comfort and discord, go for the comfort zone.

dy
everyone is ENTITLED to a struggle

02/14/2001

## don belk young

| | |
|---|---|
| **From:** | "don belk young" <donbelk@bellsouth.net> |
| **To:** | "john downey" <jjones2742@aol.com> |
| **Sent:** | Wednesday, February 14, 2001 4:39 PM |
| **Subject:** | AS ONE GREAT PHILOSOPHER SAID, "MAKE MY DAY" |

Upon reading the printed copy of the :-) :-) :-) message, it was obvious that it was truncated, especially when compared to those sent previously. So it seemed appropriate to send an addendum to "make your day." So here it is.

We have a rule that we do not go to a basketball game without tickets and they are conveniently ensconced in the upper left pocket of my shirt. The shirt will probably not pass inspection when the rest of my costume has been assembled so must remember to transfer the tickets when changing shirts.

We have experienced many firsts and have shared them with you when it seemed appropriate. So here goes. For the first time in this millennium, the green coat symbolizing faithfulness to the Blazers will be on full display this evening. The green coat has been around as long as UAB basketball. Remarkable. In all modesty, I must admit that I do make the coat look pretty good, especially if I hold in my stomach when it is buttoned. One of those little tricks that comes with maturity and superior mental skills.

And so it came to pass that another exciting day is moving right along:-.)

dy
everyone is ENTITLED to a struggle

02/14/2001

**don belk young**

| | |
|---|---|
| **From:** | "don belk young" |
| **To:** | "john downey" <jjones2742@aol.com> |
| **Sent:** | Thursday, February 15, 2001 4:04 PM |
| **Subject:** | WHAT YOU THINK I SAID |

One cannot be too careful when writing. It is important to write exactly what you want someone else to think is what you meant so that if you did not realty mean to say anything much, it would not make much difference and no one would be any worse off than they were before unless they are in that select group who have a knack for reading into whatever they see whatever they want to believe, or it may be that they do not have any idea what they want to believe without being told, in which case it would be useless to attempt to create a meaningful sentence in twenty five additional words or less. *I KNOW THAT YOU BELIEVE THAT YOU UNDERSTAND WHAT YOU THINK I WROTE, BUT AM NOT SURE THAT YOU REALIZE THAT WHAT YOU READ IS NOT WHAT I MEANT.* That just about sums it up, so let's leave it alone for awhile.

Eydie, we did get your note with the attachment with the joke about the redhead and her eyeball. And your follow-up with some clever sayings about the superior intelligence of women. I can hardly wait to forget them, so please send some more.

A baseball story got my attention in the morning paper. Mel Stottlemyre is a pitching coach for the New York Yankees and was among the first to arrive at their spring training camp in Florida. He was out all last year battling multiple myeloma. The part of his treatment plan that was mentioned was stem cell transplants. The story further said that he was in full remission.

UAB basketball went in the right direction last night. LeAndrew Bass did not play because of a "virus" or some ailment which had made him too sick to play. So after Marquette started the game with an 8-0 run, UAB played well and put up a W when it was over. A good game. The crowd continues to be disappointing.

The weekend has started. When I parked my peekup and went past the mailbox, got the mail which saved a mailbox trip, but savored the moment anyhow. If you have never savored a moment, you ought to try it sometime. Sort of like mashed potatoes with gravy. My personal favorite, though, is mashed potatoes with cream corn. Oh, yes, we were reflecting on the weekend activities. A golf game tomorrow, a wedding Saturday, and a quiet, restful day to reflect on everything on Sunday, then rest on Monday in anticipation of the beginning of another weekend next Thursday. It is amazing, the ability of the mind/brain to create positive thoughts and images.

Here is a fact that you would never know about if it was not revealed to you. I have personally solved 1001 free cell games without a loss. You might suspect that there is a gimmick in there somewhere and you would be right, but that part will not be revealed without a great of peer pressure. I have never suffered from peer pressure since I do not have any peers, and I feel pressured to say the same thing about John Downey.

Looks like a good place to STOP.
dy
everyone is ENTITLED to a struggle

02/15/2001

## don belk young

| | |
|---|---|
| **From:** | "don belk young" |
| **To:** | "john downey" <jjones2742@aol.com> |
| **Sent:** | Friday, February 16, 2001 6:07 PM |
| **Subject:** | PRESSED |

We have been oppressed, suppressed, impressed, expressed, depressed, and all the rest of the good and bad presses. It seems to be a relatively good balance so not much to complain about except when we think about it. Probably the best way to go is not to think about it, thus adroitly avoiding the dilemma and ignoring the problem if there was one. And should a problem not be there it would not make any difference anyhow so why worry.

Have just survived another storm accompanied by a two-three hour power outage. As usual, the daily excitements came streaming into our consciousness unabated and with power and forcefulness seldom experienced except when in a self-imposed state of tranquility. Such a state is difficult to obtain so when you know that you are having one you need to prolong as long as possible, and as was mentioned recently; maybe as recent as yesterday, savor the moment while you can, just like you did in the past, having been at an earlier lime. You are challenged to read anything written so far today and make any sense at all. If you can, you will be given the honor of preparing, with proper supervision, Of course, the preface to the published version of these in a limited, numbered collection. If you number these things, the idiots who buy them think that they are worth more because they are a limited edition. The real problem with this thesis is that there is an unlimited number of idiots so it's hard to know when to stop.

Recognizing that these are in a class by themself under the classification of stupid, silly nonsense I have decided to give myself a pardon while I am still in charge. Of course, I do not expect to be deposed as long as I am unopposed and as was mentioned recently there is no peer pressure, welt, you know what I think about that

I will let you know about the whimbrel. The poor thing is related to but smaller than a curlew. Some of them are called a zygodactyl because they have two pair of toes, one pair in front and the other pair in back. Like a woodpecker. Did you hear about the woodpecker that flew from Little Rock to Santa Barbara. He was heard to say a short time after he had been in his new surroundings with several colorful woodpecker concubines working on the redwoods with great success: "It's really amazing how hard your pecker gets when you are a thousand miles from home."

The power outage has been resolved. Plan to recommend to the Board of Overseers (Woowoo) that the power company be given an honorable mention for an Attaboy. Promise that no one will ever qualify for that rarefied zone that earns a matched set of Attaboys.

The Merry Go Round is getting up to full speed and it is time to get off, so bye.

dy
everyone is ENTITLED to a struggle


02/17/2001

## don belk young

| | |
|---|---|
| **From:** | "don belk young" |
| **To:** | "john downey" <jjones2742@aol.com> |
| **Sent:** | Saturday, February 17, 2001 8:56 PM |
| **Subject:** | STUMBLIN' ALONG |

On more than one occasion, we have started one of these adventures with a clear vision of what we were going to try to convey to the reader. After all, that is the purpose of written communication, i.e. to give the reader a clear straightforward statement so that she or he may reach a meaningful conclusion and think good of themselves for being so well informed. It is possible for me to understand that you, and Eydie also, might find it difficult at times to use this information in the way in which it is intended. And you would be correct. So the subject phrase of "stumblin' along" was carefully selected to characterize the artistic aspect as distinguished from the more trite and true—trite and true, how do you like that one—outcome that has become so common. Consider this opening paragraph today to be an apology for any consternation that you may have experienced because you could not distinguish between the prosaic and the artistic. If you would prefer to think that it is entirely due to your inability to appreciate art that is OK.

You know how exciting it is around here all of the time. Well, yesterday was no exception and you were the beneficiary regardless of what you thought about PRESSED. Here is the scenario. At 3:45 p.m. the lights went out, the system shut down, and the first paragraph of PRESSED was lost. We will never know the contents because even my superior mental capacity could not exactly duplicate the repartee which, of course, is of a spontaneous nature and it is not possible to duplicate spontaneity until we do a lot more work on gene control. BUT then at 5:30 the storm had passed, more or less, and the lights came on. Had to restart the Compaq and start again on PRESSED. Finished at 6:07 and sent along on its merry way. I think it travels 45,000 miles to get from here to Little Rock—22,500 miles up to something way up there, then back to earth another 22,500. Check the arithmetic if you think it necessary, but I assure that it is a total of 45,000. At 6:08 the lights went out again and everything shut down until almost dawn. So the excitement was finding the flashlight and a couple of candles so we could camp out until we decided to just sleep if out, which worked quite nicely.

One of the blessings of the storm with accompanying power outage was that we did not have to decide who was going to cook supper since there was no way to do so. We went to Backyard Burger and got a burger and milkshake, then took that with us to the Waffle House. Just a minute, there is a logical reason for such odd behavior. The burger and shake were for Davis who is pretty much in charge when he is around. Seems to have a natural talent for that. And that is what he wanted. Meantime, Woowoo wanted breakfast and my palate strongly suggested a pecan waffle. We resolved another dilemma by taking Davis' supper to the Waffle House and encountered only token resistance. The logistics were not complicated at all. The Backyard Burger and the Waffle House almost touch each other. More details will be supplied upon request.

This persiflage must stop so will stop.

dy
everyone is ENTITLED to a struggle

02/17/2001

DON YOUNG

don belk young
_____

From:       "don belk young"
To:         "john downey" <jjones2742@aol.com>
Sent:       Sunday, February 18, 2001 2:35 PM
Subject:    RAY BOOTHE IS RIGHT


**We have neglected to reflect on many of the greater philoso-
phers while reflecting on the wisdom of some of the lesser
philosophers. We have thoughtfully thought about Plato, Aristotle, Euripides. Euphrates, Socrates, Aesop and many others but have neglected the greater philos such as Mr. Ray
Boothe. Esq.**

*One of the well-known bits of wisdom imparted by Mr. Boothe,
much to his credit, recognized that you will most likely have re-
curring opportunities to contribute to the wellbeing of those to
whom you just happen to be closely related. His version of this
was "You will have more discretionary funds when your grown up
kids quit giving you an opportunity to help them."* The irony is that
he has succumbed these opportunities with much more consistency than
anyone in my circle of acquaintances—both of them. But one can always
find a way to use the wisdom of others if the LGC perform the way they
are supposed to. In one of those calls that come around supper time, and
what is so remarkable is that we may have supper anytime from 4:36 until
after midnight and it still happens at supper time. We have a standard response "We are old and rich and don't need any," or have been known
more and more frequently to just hang up. But a certain mood was prevalent when one of those calls came recently. In a word, the mood was cocky.
And it seemed like the thing to do at the time. I enlightened the person
who called about investment advice by quoting Mr. Boothe. The caller

seemed to be non-plussed. At least he did not say that he was plussed. He did not say anything for awhile, then finally asked me to repeat. If I had anything to sell, I think he would have bought it. Maybe next time.

Your note about Eydie's stem cell transplant complications just arrived. We do hope that it gets to 100% soon and say again that if you think of anything you need that we can do, we will do so quicker than you thought possible. Seriously, if we can bring or send something, please let us know. We have assumed that Henry and Michael look around the house now and then, but, again, if we can help in any way we would like to do so. Just pretend that you are some of our grown up kids and give us an opportunity.

Let me know, also, if you have noticed any dichotomous meanderings in any of this stuff. It is supposed to be that way but one has difficulty with serf critique. We have explained the misspellings and omissions every now and then so will not bother with that again. Just accept it and move on.

I have an inclination to make a loaf of bread. Sometimes this urge can be overcome by resisting the inclination so we cannot determine right now how that is going to go. I could sure use a pile of dough right now and may pretend that a bread loaf meets and exceeds such expectations. One little anecdote and we will bring this to a merciful end. Anecdote: Once upon a time, bread was divided according to status. Workers got the burnt bottom of The Loaf, the family got the middle, and guests got the top or the "upper crust." Ugh.

dy
everyone is ENTITLED to a struggle

02/18/2001

**don belk young**

From:       "don belk young"
To:         "john downey" <jjones2742@aol.com>
Sent:       Monday, February 19, 2001 2:12 PM
Subject:    ON AND ON

We have refrained from divulging the technique used in the construction of never ending sentences that ramble on and on and on and on until one would almost be berserk trying to decipher the secret method used unless the reader were fortunate enough to have a mentor who would be able, and willing, to enlighten the poor, poor confused, bewildered reader who may not even be aware that she or he had a dilemma since there are some who do not recognize a dilemma when they see one or have one and under such circumstances they would not necessarily be aware that they were not normal unless perhaps they found themselves gasping for breath, under which circumstances a normal person would begin to wonder what was going on and might look for the underlying reason for starting a paragraph

without finishing the first one not even a period or a question mark or any other punctuation marks, but even them one who has been blessed with less than average GLG capacity and is thus not responsible for anything, not to mention ones inability to discern whether they have been discriminated against or not which has been all too common a response when it is finally recognized that you have a disability and will probably get a government pension to take care of it if you-just complete the application with your name and social number, after which you will live happily ever after, even beyond the second paragraph

which also may start without the previous one ever ending because it is the prerogative of the writer to place periods and such wherever he or she wants to regardless of the rules of writing which have been put together over such a long period of time that no one can be credited with their creation, sort of like the development of mankind through the discovery of fire, the wheel, and other basics like how to get a job at LAB and other fine arts whether anyone else knows how to or not, although it needs to be admitted that there is more than. one way to be most things, however, there is a preferred way to smoke a cigar and play the piano if you do not try to do both at the same time since that would almost assuredly result in ashes from the cigar falling on the keyboard and over a long period of time would cause the piano to get out of tune and we all know that tuning a piano is almost a lost art just like putting a period at the end of a paragraph

which you cannot do if it does not coincide with the end of a sentence thus causing one to go on and on and on and on and.............................

With the greatest humility and apologies to all

dy
everyone is ENTITLED to a struggle


02/19/2001

don belk young

| | |
|---|---|
| **From:** | "don belk young" |
| **To:** | "john downey" <jjones2742@aol.com> |
| **Sent:** | Tuesday, February 20, 2001 2:51 PM |
| **Subject:** | PROBABLY |

Extensive use of the word probably is probably nothing more than a poor excuse for not knowing or, more probably, not caring. Ignorance or apathy. But we should not despair. Such characteristics abound, not in a contagious way and probably not in a genetic sense, but because we are probably too comfortable with the way things are and do not want to "rock the boat." After all, rocking the boat might cause someone to fall off, and if that should be the party of the first part it would indeed be something that we would all be better off it did not happen. That great philosopher Abe is given credit for the idea that "God must have loved the common man because he sure made a lot of them." Problem with that idea is that no one wants to be classified as "average," so mankind will continue to by to reach the next level. And we sincerely wish for everybody that they are above average. Seems only fair.

Signs of spring abound. The grass looks like it is dead, the flower bed is just plain ugly, the trees are bare, one of the outside faucets is broken and needs a part that is no longer made anywhere, the garage is cluttered, the deck really, really needs some work and some new furniture, a shingle came off the roof during the recent storm, stray dead leaves show up in odd places, dawn comes about 6 a.m. and dusk is at 6 p.m., and it seems to me, because I am known as an optimist, that all of this is a good thing because it will all get better in a relatively short time when spring arrives. We will know for sure on that very exciting day when you have to get up at 2 a.m. to change all the clocks to Daylight Saving Time.

My bathos for anticipating spring in a positive way is because it gives a valid excuse for being insincere, excessive, and insensitive, all of which seem to be very natural. Better than having mixed, uncertain and conflicting feelings, don't you think.

Just came to my attention that Republicanism is genetically determined, a very startling discovery reported on the op-ed page. This finding was greeted with relief by parents and friends of Republicans, who had blamed themselves for the political views of otherwise lovable people—their children, friends and unindicted co-conspirators. One mother, a longtime Democrat, clasped her hands in ecstasy on hearing of these findings. "I just knew it was genetic," she said, seated beside her two sons, both avowed Republicans. "I just knew nobody would actually CHOOSE that lifestyle!" The scientific community is working on a therapeutic approach to reduce, or at least control, the tendency toward a landslide of conservophobia.

As usual, we have miles to go before we sleep, and many promises to keep.

02/20/2001

## don belk young

**From:**   "don belk young"
**To:**   "john downey" <jjones2742@aol.com>
**Sent:**   Wednesday, February 21, 2001 9:59 AM
**Subject:**   RIDDLE

The answer to the riddle is that there is not an answer to the riddle because the riddle wasn't even there. Find the riddle, please, and we will find an answer, as the feller said, regardless, and even if we have to resort to efficaciousness. To be efficacious is to have the power to produce the desired result if that doesn't work, one can always try the supercilious approach. To do this, you must be capable of being contemptuous, and be full of contempt and ignorance, besides all the benefits of not knowing what you are talking or writing about while never admitting same to anyone.

UAB has a game tonight at home vs. South Florida. Woowoo wants to know how a place in Tampa can be called South Florida. Probably, there's that word again, it is so handy when you do not have a clue, probably because it is not in North Florida. But them it is not in East Florida, either. To call it West Florida does not have a good ring to it and it does not roll off the tongue. But wait! I think I have it! Yes, it is coming back thru a dim, foggy haze. At a point near what is now Sarasota, any traveler who ventured further south would be engulfed by the swampy terrain and disappear. No one ever returned. It remains a mystery to this day as to whether those unfortunates were chased by alligators (or is it crocodiles) or were transformed into a giant mosquito or possibly a manatee or one of those funny looking trees with a root system that has to be seen to be believed.

Speaking of alligators and crocodiles, did I ever relate to you the story about Professor Twist. I know I did, but you probably do not remember it, so will be glad to write it out for you if it would be helpful and add to your repertoire. You need to know something besides Dogs, Timbuktu, and a couple of limericks. If I do not hear from you, will assume that you need to know and will forward at the appropriate time. How do you know when it is appropriate, you might say. Those of us who are blessed with a superior intellect, commonly known as erudites, do not insist on always being right, but we do have a superior sense of timing for crudities and other essentials of the art of insult and being condescending. You will be pleased to know that when you are insulted in this way you may never know that it has happened.

Today should be exciting. The only reason to make such a suggestion is because each day is filled with excitement so this one should be no different. Other than doing the laundry, putting the recycle box out to picked up, calling Dr. Elkus for an appointment for Achilles tendonitis, and looking forward to the mailman's arrival, that is about it until we leave for the UAB game. One could detect a sense of excitement wondering what the food service will be at the UAB game. Since the conference USA games started, the green and gold room staff have arranged for food service at each of the games, and most of it has been quite good. Actually, it is all good, but like many other necessities (and luxuries) some are better than others. The worst we have had was _____.

John, let Eydie fill in the blank. Woowoo will probably discard this one when she comes to that part.

In all humility, your most obedient servant,

dy
everyone is ENTITLED to a struggle


02/21/2001

## don belk young

| | |
|---|---|
| **From:** | "don belk young" |
| **To:** | "john downey" <jjones2742@aol.com> |
| **Sent:** | Thursday, February 22, 2001 3:59 PM |
| **Subject:** | RIDDLE INDEED-HERE WE GO |

I SPY CRY!

*Riddle Me No Riddles*

Once upon a time, riddles were respectable. Their antiquity and function can be guessed at from the word's origin in the Old English *raedan*, 'a story or interpretation,' which is cognate with words meaning 'counsel, opinion, conjecture' and is also the origin of our modern word *read*. Such poems (for in its original form the riddle was a verse form) were a regular part of entertainment and instruction, an elevated form of guessing game. Here is one from *The Exeter Book* of about 940, in a modem translation:

> *A moth ate words. That seemed to me*
> *when I heard of that strange happening, a curious event,*
> *that the insect, a thief in darkness, devoured*
> *what was written by some man, his excellent language*
> *and its strong foundation. The thievish stranger was not*
> *at all the wiser from swallowing those words.*

[Edited and translated by WS Mackie, 1934; the answer is 'bookworm.']

However, the riddle is much more ancient than even this venerable writing. There is a story about Solomon winning a large sum of money from Hiram, King of Tyre, in a riddling contest. An Egyptian biography of the 1st century AD identifies the legendary Aesop as a former slave who went to

Babylon as riddle solver to King Lycurgus, which suggests that to be able to solve riddles was a prized skill. There is Samson's riddle in the Bible (Judges 14): "Out of the eater came forth meat / And out of the strong came forth sweetness." There is the use of riddles as a form of teaching in works such as the Jewish *Haggada*. And there is the Riddle of the Sphinx. This was the Greek one, which had the head and breasts of a woman, the body of a lion, the wings of a bird, a serpent's tail, and lion's paws, clearly a beast designed by a committee. Its name is said to come from a Greek word meaning 'to draw tight,' from which we also get the word *sphincter*, because the creature was supposed to kill by strangulation. In legend it terrorized Thebes until Oedipus could solve the riddle it propounded, at which point it killed itself by leaping off a cliff. One form of the riddle is:

> *What goes on four feet, on two feet, and three;*
> *But the more feet it goes on the weaker it be?*

Another is:

> *What has one voice,*
> *and walks on four legs in the morning,*
> *two at noon, and three in the evening?*

The answer in both cases is 'man,' who crawls on all fours as a baby, goes erect on two feet as an adult, but in old age supports himself with a staff.

Here's another English riddle:

> *Little Nancy Etticoat*
> *In a white petticoat*
> *And a red nose.*
> *The longer she stands*
> *The shorter she grows.*
>
> *[Quoted in the Encyclopaedia Britannica; the answer is 'candle.']*

In *The Hobbit*, Tolkien has Bilbo and Gollum engage in a deadly-serious riddling contest inside Goblin Mountain, of which one example is:

*It cannot be seen, cannot be felt,*
*Cannot be heard, cannot be smelt.*
*It lies behind stars and under hills*
*And empty holes it fills.*
*It comes first and follows after,*
*Ends life, kills laughter.*

[The answer is 'the dark.']

Alas, the riddle is now a debased form, more a play on words than something that demands thought and skill in its solving. Children love them, as they always have done. There was a great, but short-lived, fashion for them when I was young, which resurrected such ancient favourites as "What's green and hairy and goes up and down?" (a gooseberry in a lift) and "What's black and white and read all over" (a newspaper) which reminds me of Hilaire Belloc's Epigram "When I am dead, I hope it may be said: / 'His sins were scarlet, but his books were read.'"

Recent events in North America confirm that the riddle is far from dead. Nobody seems to be absolutely sure how it started, but quite suddenly everybody concerned with words, from librarians to newspaper columnists to dictionary makers to Usenet newsgroups such as *alt.usage.english* and *rec.puzzles* were deluged with enquiries along the lines of "There are three words in English ending in -gry. I only know hungry and angry. Please tell me what the third one is. I'm going mad trying to find the answer." The reason why so many people were tearing their hair out is that there is no third common word in English ending in -gry, though there are several rare or obsolete ones. So why were so many people desperate to find something that didn't exist?

It seems that the question had been taken from some old book of puzzles, had been given publicity, perhaps on a radio programme (Richard Lederer says it was on the Bob Grant radio talk show on WMCA in New York City in 1975), had taken the fancy of large numbers of people, and had been passed by word of mouth across North America, becoming corrupted on the way, until later hearers only received the bastardised version I've already quoted. I've seen various versions of the original form of the riddle. It may have been something like:

> *There are two words that end with "gry."*
> *Angry is one and hungry is another.*
> *What is the third word.*
> *Everyone uses it every day and*
> *Everyone knows what it means.*
> *If you have been listening,*

One of the first mistakes in transmission appears to have been the inclusion of a question mart at the end of the third line. This turned an simple bit of verbal trickery, whose answer is "what," into a fruitless exercise in lexicographic detective work. Another version is:

> *Think of words ending in 'gry.'*
> *Angry and hungry are two of them.*
> *There are only three words in the English language.*
> *What is the third word?*
> *The word is something that everyone uses every day.*
> *If you have listened carefully,*
> *I have already told you what it is.*

and in this case the answer must surely be 'language' (the third word in "the English language").

Yet a third version claiming to be the original was published in the US magazine Parade in March 1997, in a letter from Charles Wiedemann of New Jersey, who was responding to an article on the mystery by Marilyn Vos Savant. His version is:

> *There are at least three wards*
> *in the English language that end in g or y.*
> *One of them is "hungry," and another one is "angry."*
> *There is a third word, a short one,*
> *which you probably say every day.*

*If you are listening carefully to everything I say,*
*you just heard me say it three times.*
*What is it?*

which relies on verbal trickery to confuse the quickly said "g or y" with "gry." The answer is actually 'say.'

In one form or another the basic riddle seems to have been known for many years (one person, identified only as <jackper@aol.com> is quoted in the *alt.usage.english* FAQ as saying "I heard this riddle 20 years ago from a fiddle player. He got it from his wife who taught pre-school"). Several librarians in the US report that it is a common question, to which long ago they determined stock answers, confirming that it is far from new. It seems it has also crossed the Atlantic, as it is quoted as a question asked of the Oxford Word and Language Service (OWLS) in *Questions of English*.

Everybody is very pleased that this most recent peak of interest in the riddle is now over and we can get back to some real work. Here, for the record and in case anybody is still interested, are a few other words in *-gry* that do exist in English, though only specialist dictionary-makers and students of the history of the language have even heard of most of them. I have left out compounds such as *land-hungry*,

| *aggry* | Coloured and variegated glass beads of ancient manufacture, found buried in the ground in Africa. A word of unknown origin. Seemingly always used attributively, as in *aggry* beads. |
| --- | --- |
| *braggry* | A variant form of *braggery*. Obsolete. |
| *conyngry* | An obsolete dialectal variant of *conyger*, itself an obsolete |

02/23/2001

## don belk young

| | |
|---|---|
| **From:** | "don belk young" |
| **To:** | "gloria" <gwalker@uabmc.edu> |
| **Cc:** | "john downey" <jjones2742@aol.com> |
| **Sent:** | Thursday, February 22, 2001 4:10 PM |
| **Subject:** | WITH APOLOGIES AGAIN |

Hey, sorry about that thing about riddles that is too long for anyone's attention span, but do the best you can with it. Comes under the heading of "If you do not want to know the answer, don't ask the question." All I did was type gry into the search box and there it was.

John, will get back to the regular order of business tomorrow. Tallahassee is still high on the list of things that need to be explained. Gloria, this has nothing to do with the 2000 election problems in Florida.

Are you about ready to try the Bright Star?

dy
everyone is ENTITLED to a struggle

02/23/2001

**don belk young**

| | |
|---|---|
| **From:** | "don belk young" |
| **To:** | "john downey" <jjones2742@aol.com> |
| **Sent:** | Friday, February 23, 2001 1:41 PM |
| **Subject:** | PROFESSOR TWIST |

You asked for it and now you are going to get it. Sounds threatening. Do not despair. You will be able to handle it. Just exercise some of your prerogatives and maintain the proper respect not to mention your perspective which must be in reasonably good condition to endure one of these. With the practice you have had recently, should be a piece of cake. Or pie. Or a piece of something. But first (remember how we explored the use of "but" to start a sentence) some background is necessary to be better prepared so that you will have a full appreciation of the wisdom and humor that might escape otherwise. And one does not want to let wisdom and humor get away or get lost or be wasted.

So here is the preparation. You have experienced, on both sides of the desk, the thing known as pedantry. A professor is both erudite, by his own standards, and is an egotist from the standpoint that he thinks that he knows everything, and that the lesser, wannabe erudites need to be enlightened. Also, the natural tendency of many so-called teachers to be what is commonly known as pompous from time to time, that is to say, most of the time, or many would say, all the time.

So here we go with "Professor Twist."

> *I give you now Professor Twist,*
> *A most respected scientist*
> *His Board says, "He never bungles"*
> *And sends him off to foreign jungles.*

*One night while camped by the riverside*
*He suddenly missed his brand new bride.*

*She was, his guide told him much later*
*Eaten by an alligator.*

*The professor could not help but smile.*
*"YOU MEAN," he said "A CROCODILE."*

Now you have another item for your repertoire. It will take about five minutes to commit to memory. With advance permission, Eydie will surely be a willing audience. With a little practice, she will probably be able to prompt you when you are about to go astray. You two could have been Burns and Allen with a little practice.

Have not talked with Ray or Jan for about a week, so do not have an update. I think we will hear from Cheryl should anything eventful occur, but will give them a call soon. Their address for regular mail is: 4244 Shiloh, zip code 35213. They do not have email, but I am sure that Tom and Cheryl do and will try to get that.

The Blazers did well at South Florida and at home against Memphis but lost both games. This week they have lost by 17 at Memphis, and South Florida won the game here on our home court by a score of 75-47. It was almost cruel to watch. USF used a trapping zone defense and UAB players acted like it was a complete mystery. In a word, it was awful. They are on their way to Depaul and Louisville before playing their final game of the year here against St. Louis on March 3. I do not believe that they will play any games after that until next November.

EVERYONE does need a struggle. You should have one sometime and it will be an epiphanious experience. Guaranteed.

02/23/2001

**don belk young**

| | |
|---|---|
| **From:** | "don belk young" |
| **To:** | "john downey" \<jjones2742@aol.com\> |
| Sent | Saturday, February 24, 2001 7:17 PM |
| **Subject:** | IT'S ABOUT TIME |

UAB managed to win at Depaul. There is a very good reason for this result. When the game was over, UAB had more points than DePaul. We lost the first half by ten points, then scored the first ten points in the second half to get even, then went ahead, and never looked back, as they say. David Walker, the best defensive player could not play, neither could Tony Johnson, the best basketball savvy guy on the team, and Bass fouled out with about ten minutes to play. It was strange to watch—we saw it on Channel 2 (68) in Birmingham. My prediction remains that we are not going anywhere post season. Auburn lost a close one to Mississippi and Alabama was walloped by Florida,

Question. Would you rather be glabrous or glabrate? Answer. Depends. Corollary question? Would you rather be hairless or almost hairless? It is possible to become glabrous over time and will almost certainly happen if you are glabrescent. Just keep all of this in mind when it comes up in a casual conversation. You will never need it in a serious conversation so do not worry about not remembering it when you need it unless, perchance, you think you are having a casual conversation and it is really more serious, Should this happen, start coughing and rush to the bathroom. Stay as long as necessary and, sure enough, when you return you will only be asked how you are and you will have changed the subject successfully.

About changing the subject. It is about time to get serious about this Tallahassee business. We—my editor and publisher and assorted assistants— are continuing research on this very important revelation, but the revelation continues to not be revealed. We expect a breakthrough but we have no idea when that is likely to occur. Right now the approach is to study the anatomy of the word. Looking at it straight on, the first word is Tall, then a, then has, then see. Very logical so far. The problem is. "What do we do now, coach." We refuse to let the absence of any kind of solution, logical or otherwise, deter our determination to determine what to do next, and will probably, there's that convenient word again, not determine what to do next until we have determined the next step.

About time to start the weekend, so adios and all that.

dy
everyone is ENTITLED to a struggle

**don belk young**

| | |
|---|---|
| **From:** | "don belk young" |
| **To:** | "john downey" <jjones2742@aol.com> |
| **Sent:** | Sunday, February 25, 2001 6:50PM |
| **Subject:** | THE DIFFERENCE |

The difference is in the diffidence. If you say you can't tell the difference, then you have not been paying attention because there is a lot of difference in many different things. Usually when there is present more than one thing, there is a difference. The way to prove such an assumption would be to get two different things in the same place at the same time and look at them while they were standing still. You could make observations while they were moving but would not be able to present an iron clad, bullet proof case. In the final analysis, as was pointed in the sixth word, the dominance of the diffidence would be likely to prevail. Let's just think out loud here for a moment and try to think of a way to present this theorem without having to use a syllogism; deductive reasoning, or a specious argument. To refresh you on use of specious, it is a technique used mostly by liberals to make something seem to be true, but it is false or deceptive. That is not what we are trying to do here.

We are searching for an easy to understand phrase or a simple truism that would demystify "the difference is in the diffidence." What about "Let us not judge them too harshly in this season of mercy and forgiveness." Problem with that is that it has a touch of pomposity and high handedness, which is what we are trying to avoid at all cost We dealt with that in a previous essay.

Let us continue in a relaxed mode and just trust the LGC. We know that there is a way to deal with diversity and perplexity at the same time. Any scholar, as attested by philosophers from Aristotle to Zygebo, would agree with this basic assumption. This cannot be confirmed because neither A or Z can be reached before I have to complete this piece.

But we digress. Let's see now. How about, uh, wait, I think I have it. And after two or three seconds of deep and thoughtful thought, it is my humble suggestion that we use the simple, eloquent phrase "**Don't sweat the small stuff!!**"

That'll have to do for today.

dy
everyone is ENTITLED to a struggle

02/25/2001

## don belk young

| | |
|---|---|
| **From:** | "don belk young" |
| **To:** | "john downey" <jjones2742@aol.com> |
| **Sent:** | Monday, February 26, 2001 9:10 PM |
| **Subject:** | ALMOST |

We had almost decided to go to Lovoy's when we almost got ran off the road because we did not see the car that almost ran us off the road. Then we proceeded to almost get lost on the way from the Eastern section, more commonly known as the areas near Mountain Brook; to Southside. We almost made it all the way through UAB without someone challenging our right to the left lane.

Then we almost got to Lovoy's before we decided that we were almost home so went on and now am almost finished with this one but will finish tomorrow and will never bother to explain.

dy
everyone is ENTITLED to a struggle

02/27/2001

**don belk young**

| | |
|---|---|
| **From:** | "don belk young" |
| **To:** | "john downey" <jjones2742@aol.com> |
| **Sent:** | Tuesday, February 27, 2001 5:28 PM |
| **Subject:** | FAT TUESDAY |

Fat Tuesday has a nice sound, and it is between morbid Monday and woeful Wednesday and two days before thunderous Thursday. Everyone should be thrilled to be able to think about what any other kind of Tuesday might be. If one would be sort of pusillanimous about it, it might go away and not come back until 2002.

You may have noticed that ALMOST, yesterday's production, almost amounted to nothing. It was a result of the events of the day which resulted in not enough of anything to do much. So we just sent along some blathering about ALMOST, which was inspired by some country western song sung by a country western singer. Should you have to know or need to know for any reason, will have some research done to find out who was singing about being ALMOST PERSUADED. We are willing to do that because we are egalitarian and besides, believe in equality. The principle is that all people are equal and should enjoy equal social, political and economics rights and opportunities. It is the stuff that politicians and motivational speakers get downright emotional about. They are the same class of people who can't tell a clavicle from an infarction, and can be downright unequivocal about it, in a Biblical sense.

UAB @ Louisville tonight. In any previous year, this one could be written down as L, but Danny Crum is having about as much trouble winning as Murry Bartow this year. Gary Sanders will probably get preempted by George Bush, but maybe George will make a short speech. John, I am going to try to include part of a diary that is on the computer somewhere. If I can find it and copy it, will send along.

January 12, 1935

At 4 a.m. the gravel rattling at the upstairs window woke us. Frank said "It's your turn" and he turned over and pulled the covers to his side of the bed. COLD COLD COLD jumped out of the feather bed. The winter underwear that I had slept in was quickly covered with a denim shirt, another shirt, a pair of bib overalls, and heavy socks. None of the bedrooms upstairs had any heat source. The only heat in the house was in the big wood burning stove in the room next to the kitchen. The fire in the kitchen range would die out after the water had been heated to wash dishes after supper.

But the fire in the big stove was kept burning by adding wood at bedtime—8 p.m., which would be used but would have enough embers to start again at about 4 a.m. when Dad got up—he and Mom had a downstairs bedroom. And Dad had added some wood and poked the fire to get it started as part of the morning routine. Then he had started for the cowbarn, and on his way tossed the gravel to rattle on the upstairs bedroom window to wake us.

At this time Dad and I were up; Mom and Frank and Gay would be up and about in due time. The cold had invaded everything during the night and the stove was just beginning to provide warmth— if you got close enough.

Ran downstairs in the dark. Did not use lamps or candles to get dressed since it was a very simple process of putting on the clothes that you had taken off when you went to bed. I had left my shoes next to the stove so that they could start to warm up when the fire was started. But they were stiff and cold anyhow. Put the shoes on the top of the stove for a minute or two while buttoning shirts and getting dressed. Grab shoes and put on quickly. The hot shoes felt good. Smell of warm leather. Hope Mom doesn't notice or does not say anything if she does. She would light a coal oil lamp first thing when she got up to start a fire in the kitchen stove and start fixing breakfast and school lunches.

Gloves, coat, cap with pull down ear flaps and hanging on a nail. Turn coat collar up, ear flaps down, put on overshoes on the porch (they are always muddy and covered with whatever was last stepped in around the barn) and out the door, barn is about 100 yards walk. Dad has started feeding horses and cows. When it is this cold, the animals stay in the barn at night—horses in stalls, cows in stanchions. With a stanchion a cow can lay down or get up but cannot move around. Horses can move around their stalls when awake. (They sleep standing up with their knees locked.)

In the cowbarn, constant attention is required for sanitation, but we called it something else then. Anyhow we shovel.

02/27/2001

## don belk young

| | |
|---|---|
| **From:** | "don belk young" |
| **To:** | "john downey" <jjones2742@aol.com> |
| **Sent:** | Wednesday, February 28, 2001 8:31 PM |
| **Subject:** | YESTERDAY |

You received enough in yesterday's email to keep you busy for two days so we will offer just one brief item today. A sign in California says "Due to a severe shortage of electricity, the light at the end of the tunnel has been turned off." Never could find it anyhow.

dy
everyone is ENTITLED to a struggle

03/01/2001

## don belk young

| | |
|---|---|
| **From:** | "don belk young" |
| **To:** | "john downey" <jjones2742@aol.com> |
| **Sent:** | Thursday, March 01, 2001 4:22 PM |
| **Subject:** | KUDOS |

Have you ever had a kudo. There are some that would say that an Attaboy is in that category. I will explain that when it seems like the proper thing to do, which may never happen. After all, to be given praise, credit, or glory for an achievement may be superfluous. Those of us who are blessed with a sense of self-importance do not need a kudo to know what we know or do not know, not to mention other things that may or may not be of some insignificance. There are times when it seems more rewarding to participate in the sport of camogie, or perhaps bask in one's own effulgence, a brilliant light radiating from something. It does not count if your effulgence is from your own halo.

Eydie, got your update report and will take the optimistic view that you will be commuting from Birmingham to Little Rock about once a month. The sooner the better. And we know where all the corners are, at La Dolce Vita, Bright Star, Villa Rosa, not to mention Lovoy's and other places of lesser reputation. We have become aficionados of the Waffle House, and can certify that they do not have any out of the way corners. Corners they've got, but they are not the right kind. Also for you, Eydie, this one is being recirculated and should not be used in everyday casual conversations. But here goes. What do you get when you cross a lying politician with a corrupt attorney? Answer: Chelsea. And this answer does not refer to that town between Hugh Daniel Drive and Harpersville. No. Not at all.

John, in previous essays we (editorially speaking) have defended mispelings and omisions (notice the clever reference to misspelling and omissions—my spellchecker will have a field day), but have withheld from you explanation so that you could properly savor the rush of understanding when we disclose what this process is called. It is the art of being caco-graphical—i.e., indulging in bad handwriting or misspelling. Also known as the evil spirit called cacodemon.

UAB, talk about a yo-yo basketball season. When we are supposed to completely fall apart because we demonstrated that we know how to lose when we have a ten point lead in the second half, lo and behold, we man-age to win two on the road, including Louisville. So we will have St. Louis here Saturday night and the suspense creates more emotion than one can handle under any circumstance, and especially so if the catered food before the game is below standard. But since I have no standards in that regard, we will disregard any reference to the texture of the celery and eat the damn stuff anyhow, then see what happens in the gymna-sium, or whatever they call that place where those guys go around bounc-ing a big round ball.

John, do you know what something called the Honorary letters club is about? Much to my surprise, one of the walls on the concourse has pictures of persons who have been involved somehow in the athletic program. Gene Bartow is the first, dated circa 1978, and others follow in some order. But I never heard of it until this year and do not anything about it. As you know from a careful study of the content of these essays, it is extremely unusual for this writer, editor, publisher, proofreader to not be in complete control of whatever it is convenient to be in control of, so this has been somewhat disconcerting to me when my fans approach me with extended pencils and ask me to write on something. Fortunately, this has not actually happened, but one's mind goes out in all directions with wonderment about how to handle this situation should it occur, Your advice would be appreciated. I would be receptive to a suggestion to "forget it." But should you feel to give such advice, it would be appreciated if you could think some way to convey the meaning without a direct statement. Must think about feelings, you know.

We hope to see you soon. And we are unanimous in that!!!!!!!!!

dy
everyone is ENTITLED to a struggle

03/01/2001

**don belk young**

From:      "don belk young"
To:        "john downey" <jjones2742@aol.com>
Sent:     Friday, March 02, 2001 11:54 AM
Subject:   NEVER TALK ABOUT THE WEATHER

Never talk about the weather. it is a useless exercise in small talk. Can you remember any occasion when you could classify speculation about rain or sunshine, etc. as large talk. Thought so. More about that later.

Superfluous. Do you pronounce the first "u" as "you," or do you elide and skip it altogether.

Back to the weather, and whether the weather is worth wasting words and thoughts on, or whether the weather would be the same if one chose to ignore any discussion. Perhaps the best approach is to use it to fill those blank spaces that seem to occur with considerable regularity in everyday conversation. An attack of aposiopesis, for example, would require some response. Should this occur, it would be rude for one to just stare at the aposiopesistic. Rather, it would be quite appropriate to diplomatically make a comment about the clouds or sunshine or anything to help the person who has been suddenly afflicted with a break in speaking to recover. Certain individuals who shall remain nameless (because we cannot remember who they are right now) would never have this problem, yet one should be prepared for such a situation.

One thing worse than idle talk about the weather is writing some nonsensical thesis about the uselessness of talking about it. This, too, should be avoided at all costs. Careful research has not revealed any prohibition, quite the opposite, something called "free speech." This phrase has been interpreted to include so-called writing, but it is difficult, indeed, to think of writing as speech. Best thing to do, under such circumstances, is take a low profile and get out of the way of any flying objects hurled by irate readers and listeners.

We are going to some sort of reception honoring Gene Bartow tonight and will be in attendance for the last game of the season tomorrow night. Wish you were here.

A final reminder. Never talk or write about the weather. It is an awful bore and serves no useful purpose, as a general rule, which is the best kind.

dy
everyone is ENTITLED to a struggle

03/02/2001

**don belk young**

From:      "don belk young"
To:        "john downey" <jjones2742@aol.com>
Sent:     Saturday, March 03, 2001 3:16 PM
Subject:   LEFTOVERS

OF ALL THE THINGS I HAVE LOST
I MISS MY MIND THE MOST

Today we will bring together all those things that have been apart or not to-gether before. What they are are left over notes from these writing experi-ences that have not been used. The way to tell which ones have been used is if they are no longer here. They have been discarded, thrown into the dustbin or ashcan or whatever our British ancestors call those things where you put rubbish or trash. These will be listed in random order and will not be com-mented In much detail unless it seems like an interesting thing to do.

A caconym is an incorrect name, Example: John Jones.

Cacology is poor use or choice of words. A lot of that going around.

July 2, 1982 is the anniversary date for the first day of work for Edna at Lovoy's.

Richard Alan Elkus is the name of my Achilles tendon doctor. His phone no. is here also but you do not need it (available upon re-quest).

Can you have a plain, unadulterated ectomy? I have heard of tonsil, adenoid, hyster. Is that all there is?

Can one ask himself or herself or itself a rhetorical? Does it fade away if you do not answer? What if you answer it but do not say anything out loud? Did anyone hear? If not, has it really been an-swered? Deep stuff, yep, about knee deep and needs to be shoveled out the door, over the threshold. Remind to remind you to tell you how thresholds came to be. Clue: It was to keep

the thresh from sliding outside, i.e. to **hold the thresh**.

Time to change the upstairs filter. This note has been on my desk upstairs for about three weeks, but the filter is in the garage, well, nuff said.

Hadrian's wall is in Great Britain.

Wrote about the weather yesterday but did not say anything about it. It rained.

Our neighbor brought some oatmeal cake recently, so we have obtained the recipe, which I thoughtfully send to you by separate email.

The petty cash fund owes me $13.60.

Just received your email including the attachment from your son in law. Had mixed results working with the attachment. First the click on the paper clip went to a blank page, then got a short note about the funny attachment, but did not find a way to open it.

We are ready to celebrate your return to B'ham whenever that occurs. Hope you get the right numbers on the 9th.

You must have sent Rep. Burton a copy of your note to me. A message on our answering machine was somewhat muddled and muffled but sounded like he was saying that he would look into UAB finances during the 70's/80's as soon as they get the tax cut passed. Perhaps we shall have our 15 seconds of fame, after all.

The exit today will crepuscular, like twilight, resembling the fading light of dusk.

dy
everyone is ENTITLED to a struggle

03/03/2001

## don belk young

| | |
|---|---|
| **From:** | "don belk young" |
| **To:** | "john downey" <jjones2742@aol.com> |
| **Sent:** | Sunday, March 04, 2001 4:08 PM |
| **Subject:** | AND THEN THERE WERE NONE |

You may have seen it, you may have heard about it, you may have read about it, but no one has been able to find a way to put a positive spin on the outcome of St Louis v. UAB last night. In a word, it was awful. Ben Younger and we were the only people who bothered to spend any time in the G&G after the game. So we are off to Louisville to play Louisville on Wed. nite and then we can start talking about next year.

On a more positive note, the weather, which we do not talk about or write about, could be worse. Should you ask how it could be worse, we should not put a positive spin on that either. But it's a thought. As one of those famous philosophers said "I know that someday the sun is bound to shine" and he seemed believable at the time.

Well, the usual excitement. We went to church to watch Davis and Haley and Emily be part of a musical ensemble called The Joyful Noise. Then on to AVCC for buffet. At home the doorbell has been ringing incessantly—two times in an interval of less than one hour. A Girl Scout delivered some cookies and lightened the billfold by $6. Shortly thereafter Ann Cooke came by with a bottle of wine to bribe me to fill out a form to rollover. I told her that my ankles were too tense to do a pain free rollover. What we mean is that we filled out a form to rollover a 401k to an IRA. Ms. Cooke is now on her way to Homewood and we are contemplating turning on the TV to pretend to watch a basketball game while resting the eyelids. It's a trick that comes in handy two or three times a day, especially when you have tired of playing solitaire dawn, with a deck of fifty-one while watching Captain Kangaroo.

Do you know any doggerel. Or is that something you make up when you need to and have nothing better to do. Once upon a time my friend Alva Booher, you do not know him, would recite a piece that started thus: "The barefoot boy with shoes on, stood sitting on the street," and that is all I can remember. May be a good thing, what some would call a blessing. It sort of sends the LGC antigoglin just trying to deal with it

Opened the quotation book at random and here it is: "If there is no Hell, a good many preachers are obtaining money under false pretenses." Compliments of Billy Sunday.

About unrequited: is that something that we all have or does it need to be acquired through persistence, perspiration, hard work and luck. Must be an abstract concept of some sort that has escaped our attention so far. If you get some and find that it is a good thing, let me have some if it is fungible. Money is fungible, boards are not. Again, should you require a full explanation of any thing that may have gone heretofore or occur hereafter, all you have to do is ask. We will not be haughty and make you wish that you had not asked even if we wanted to. It is part of our self-discipline that governs day to day behavior in a most sensible way. This last paragraph got in here by mistake so just skip it if you want to.

As they say at the end of Mississippi, I comeuh for the lasta time.

dy
everyone is ENTITLED to a struggle

03/04/2001

## don belk young

| | |
|---|---|
| **From:** | "don belk young" |
| **To:** | "john downey" <jjones2742@aol.com> |
| **Sent:** | Monday, March 05, 2001 12:25 PM |
| **Subject:** | VICISSITUDES |

It's about time that we had a change in our vicissitudes, don't you think. Or perhaps that is something that can be exercised on an intermittent basis. When I found that a vicissitude was something unexpected, perhaps a change in ones fortunes, a series of thoughts, one at a time, in random order, started racing around pretty much out of control. One footnote type of thought wondered whether it was possible to have a vicissitude if you did not already have a fortune. Then it was revealed that a fortune could go in either direction. One that went in the wrong direction is called a misfortune. It then became clear that you can have a vicissitude no matter what. Our best hope is that they occur on a highly random selective basis and do not bother us on a day to day basis.

The admonishment about weather talk still applies, so will not tell you that it is unseasonably cold here today. We have three kinds of unpronounceable plants, not including the dianthus, that are emerging along with Bradford pear blossoms and tulip trees, but this type of weather should not be a problem. Besides, it is good for the peach crop. Do you like peaches? I'll give you the last word.

The Jones File may need a part-time librarian to manage the information and maintain the files. One requirement of any applicant is that they will be able to store these valuable writings so that they will not from the ravages of time. Question: Why should an inanimate object like a piece of paper be entitled to preservation forever and not have to suffer from ravages, when we are very much aware that humans deal with ravages on a regular basis? Must be an opportunity in there somewhere. One of my philosopher acquaintances used his entire five minute seminar one time trying to convince the skeptics in the class that a "problem" should be viewed as an opportunity. He was at a disadvantage because he was the final raconteur of the day. The class had been learning the art of beer drinking during a tong afternoon session and everyone had a short attention span due to some pithy messages from the bladder.

Do you think it is time for an index of the subjects dealt with in these essays. The index could use brief explanations of each subject title to help the reader find an area of interest. A disclaimer could be made that if one did not want to read any of it, it would not be entered on her permanent record.

Santana High School in Santee, California has just entered our consciousness because of a shooting, apparently one of the students. Several injured. Bad news.

dy
everyone is ENTITLED to a struggle

03/05/2001

## don belk young

| | |
|---|---|
| **From:** | "don belk young" |
| **To:** | "john downey" <jjones2742@aol.com> |
| **Sent:** | Tuesday, March 06, 2001 1:56 PM |
| **Subject:** | WHAT TIME IS IT |

The fingertips are on the keyboard but nothing is happening. Also seem to be having an attack of MEGO right here in the middle of the day. Aha! What is happening is that nothing is happening. But we always have a great deal of excitement sometime each day. Have already been to the mailbox and put out the trash, so that has been the highlight of the day to this point. But the main event is about to unfold right before our eyes, We just have not yet sensed the presence of heightened awareness that should accompany the preparation of a proem. Do not, repeat do not, jump to a conclusion about proem. It is not supposed to be poem. There is madness to this method and we can prove, beyond a reasonable doubt, that the diameter of the obtuse is = to pie are square.

We were at the office of Dr. McClain yesterday to find out the results. of several tests that Woowoo has been undergoing. The diagnosis is LUPUS so we have started the learning process about what this is and how to deal with it. So that's what time it is. It is time to look at the medical dictionary and computer websites and see what we can find out about this.

Just had an inspiration about WHAT TIME IS IT. It is time to take a nap so will write again as soon as 1 have a full recovery and regain capacity to create something from nothing. This one is about as close to creating nothing from something as you will ever be privileged to witness first or second hand.

So you should just accept it for what it is worth. See how easy it is.

dy
everyone is ENTITLED to a struggle

03/06/2001

## don belk young

| | |
|---|---|
| **From:** | "don belk young" |
| **To:** | "john downey" <jjones2742@aol.com> |
| **Sent:** | Wednesday, March 07, 2001 12:31 PM |
| **Subject:** | NOW WHAT |

Thanks for your email. We appreciate your concern, and will really appreciate any research results about LUPUS. It has been diagnosed as systemic, which can apparently be quite pervasive. Several different body systems may be affected—the skin, joints, kidneys, nervous system, lungs, heart and/or blood-forming organs. Like most medical problems, it will not necessarily affect everyone the same way. So we will be finding out more on a day to day basis and continue on the exciting journey, including daily trips to the mailbox. We do not have the same amount of excitement that you do in the mailbox scenario since our mailbox is only about 22 steps away, and you must get to walk about 68 steps one way. We know that you will be glad to experience your daily travels when you are back in Birmingham, excuse me, Mountain Brook. Or as we say in our trailer park, NOW WHAT.

Would have gone to AVCC for some golf, but still have problems with Achilles tendonitis, now complicated by a sore throat, clogged ears, difficulty swallowing, a runny nose, a bad disposition, chronic misbehavior, and generally frumpy, unattractive, drab and dowdy. The good part is that you would never know it if you had the privilege of being in my presence because, in ways known only to a select few, I am able to ignore all of these ailments and concentrate on the good stuff. It just happens that there is not very much good stuff available on short notice so a disclaimer is in order and I hereby proclaim a disclaimer that will absolve both of us for improper, indecent or insidious behavior, including misspelled words, etc.

The trick is to be omniscient when it is necessary or convenient to do so. So THAT'S WHAT right now.

By the way, if you do now know or have not had the experience of omniscience, you should try it. You will learn to be more egotistical than the ordinary, everyday person. It will waste less of your time getting people to dislike you—they will be able to take an instant dislike, thus conserving both your time and energy, not to mention the angst that tends to rile the liver and overload the bladder. These maladies, especially the latter, have unlimited potential for creating confusion and embarrassment for all involved, especially the party of the first part. By the time that has been completed, the party of the last part will not have any idea whether they are even in the ballgame, not to mention whether it is their turn to bat. They are likely to be bewildered and will be seen to be wandering around like Moses, lost and muttering NOW WHAT. Did Moses ever explain why it took him forty years to figure out that he was lost. I would bet that he went past at least one camel refueling station every day and never asked directions the first time.

A major victory today. Have been trying to get my Medicare card renewed since the unfortunate incident in Fairfield. Each time the round and round stuff about pushing telephone buttons ended with frustration and failure. Woowoo took charge and found the website address and, sure enough, with step by step instruction, much like driving from here to the Food World store, it was about a ten minute process to get written confirmation that a renewal would be mailed within 30 days. So my calendar is marked for April 7 with a note "Medicare card not received, NOW WHAT."

As that famous philosopher Mussolini said just before the gallows door was opened "NOW WHAT."

WHEW!!!!! I'm glad that's over. How about you…+++++++"""""""" :-) dy

dy
everyone is ENTITLED to a struggle

03/07/2001

## don belk young

| | |
|---|---|
| **From:** | "don belk young" |
| **To:** | "john downey" <jjones2742@aol.com> |
| **Sent:** | Thursday, March 08, 2001 8:07 PM |
| **Subject:** | WATCHING THE GAME |

Since we have nothing else to do, it seemed like the thing to do at the time, now, to see UAB and Cincinnati. So far so good. Arnold just made a three pointer to put UAB ahead. And we are now ahead by 5 points with about six minutes to go.

But we must not allow ourselves to get involved with such mundane activities as a routine basketball game. There must be about forty two games being played today and the total already finished is not something that your everyday bookkeeper would be able to work up any sweat over.

No, let us wander around and find something to postulate about. Problem with that idea is that postulating is being very elusive this evening. It is just one of those times when more than one thing is happening at the same time and none of them are significant to be given any serious attention so not much of anything is being accomplished. Wandering around, we touched on that 40 year wandering without asking for directions last time. Upon further thought it is not at all surprising. Moses was just being Moses, that's all I say. And more power to us all for his leadership.

Think it is about time to look for something mellifluous. Maybe that would have the desired result by establishing an aura of calmness that right now is not here at all, not even in disguise.

dy
everyone is ENTITLED to a struggle

03/08/2001

## don belk young

| | |
|---|---|
| **From:** | "don belk young" |
| **To:** | "john downey" <jjones2742@aol.com> |
| **Sent:** | Friday, March 09, 2001 314 PM |
| **Subject:** | HOW ABOUT SOME TAIHOA |

Buster, my horse, would always stop when he knew that I wanted him to, and he could tell by my body language. Most of us, especially those that read stories about people stopping horses, think you stop a horse by saying "Whoa." Even if you said it out load, it would sound like WO. That it is how we would get a horse or horses to stop in the Midwest. We would pull on the reins at the same time, with as much force as necessary to get the message to the animals. It is essential that man maintain his mastery over animals (at the present time, that does not include women, quite the contrary, man is used in an all-inclusive sense to mean mankind which so far includes women and children). Taihoa is just one version of a similar circumstance; just slow down, be patient, do not hurry. Taihoa would be used only when Whoa did not work. Only the most punctilious and fastidious would take such great care about such small details, commonly known as the small stuff, about which you should not sweat.

Apologies for yesterday. We must have these experiences once in awhile to keep things in perspective. Edgar Allen Poe suffered from such a malady every day except for the time that he did the Raven thing. And Walt Whitman had a couple of days when he could not think up a single rhyme. Actually, he wrote the kind of poetry that does not rhyme so avoided the problem altogether.

All in all, it was not much of a day except for the effort that UAB put forth in Louisville. Good show.

Looking back to the reference to camel refueling stations, I must admit that I did not have any idea what we were talking about, just seemed logical that the circumstances Moses found himself in would have been in an environment and culture that would have extensive camel facilities. They would have referred to them as hoobahs, or poobahs, or maybe hookahs, but as long as we know what was the general meaning, it does not really matter.

To put in place some of the principles that are so firmly embedded in these essays that they cannot be found, the time is approaching when it may be necessary to issue a manifesto that will proclaim in uncertain terms what the real meaning of this stuff is about. Such a manifesto would need to be accompanied by a statement of policy accompanied by clearly stated objectives. You cannot have a strategy without a tactic because it would be imprudent and impudent to do so. There was a time when you could be rather careless about such an undertaking but that would not be in good taste.

We believe that the potential readership should want to have the option to continue to be confused and uncertain in the face of facts to the contrary, no matter what. It is just easier to be stupid than it is to try to do something about it. To many it is a right and a privilege to flaunt ones lack of privileges, also known as victimhood. It must be "guaranteed" by an amendment to something like the Constitution. We will be more obtuse about all this when the manifesto is ready for publication.

And do not forget about Tallahassee. There has got to be an explanation and we intend to invent one at the proper time and in a manner in keeping with the good intentions of as many as can be enlisted.

Arriverdici!!!!...................................................................dy

dy
everyone is ENTITLED to a struggle

03/09/2001

**don belk young**

| | |
|---|---|
| **From:** | "don belk young" |
| **To:** | "john downey" <jjones2742@aol.com> |
| **Sent:** | Saturday, March 10, 2001 12:27 PM |
| **Subject:** | THE OTHER WAY |

The other way is better. One becomes accustomed to doing something in a certain way and finds it difficult, nay, impossible, to try another way. This is only an observation and is unrelated to any recent experiences so do not try to read anything between the lines. Frankly, that between the lines stuff tends to be unbelievable. It seems more like the reader wants a certain outcome so explains her conclusion by saying that she could read between the lines. It is another of taking literary license, much like placing an umlaut above a vowel. You have seen those two little dots over a vowel. Would place one here but do not know how to do that so will not put one here. Pretty straightforward logic there. The umlaut is put in place over a vowel to show you that it—the vowel—is pronounced differently from the way it is pronounced. I got lost, too, so if you are suffering from temporary or permanent bewilderment, you are in good company.

Frankly, it would be more appropriate to furcate the vowel or anything else that was making things so complicated that you could not cope. Wups, maybe we meant bifurcate. That is how you make two things out of one and an umlauted vowel could not be any more than some sort of literary bifurcation. Some authors will do anything to get attention.

Thanks for the reference to information about Lupus. It has been extremely helpful in our understanding the symptoms, diagnosis, treatment, prognosis, etc. Woowoo is scheduled to see Dr. Boulware next week and we hope to get a better handle on how to proceed.

We enjoyed everything about the UAB/Cincinnati game except the outcome. My observation was that Igor should not have waited until his last game to display his talent. As we said previously, wait next year.

The weekend is underway and excitement abounds. The cat has been out the back door, then in the back door, then out the front door so logic would say that she is now out front. And she is running around naked with not a bit of frippery. Cats are bad to do that. The mailperson has been here today so that has been attended to. We did breakfast at breakfast time, and must see what's for lunch soon. TV has so much basketball going on that it seems that a good term for such goings on would be "March Madness," or did someone already think about that?

May try a little golf this afternoon to test the Achilles tendon. Follow up with Dr. Elkus next week on that rehabilitation project. The trick is to walk until just before the aches begin. Perhaps can learn how to do that with enough practice.

We are ready for you-all to return. We live by the lake, so if you are going by, just drop in.

dy
everyone is ENTITLED to a struggle

03/11/2001

## don belk young

| | |
|---|---|
| **From:** | "don belk young" |
| **To:** | "john downey" <jjones2742@aol.com> |
| **Sent:** | Sunday, March 11, 2001 11:08 AM |
| **Subject:** | :-) GOOD NEWS, YES INDEED :-) |

Usually takes a little longer to remember to go to the email box on Sunday. But the note from you that you will be back in Birmingham by next weekend is the best news we have had since November 27. Even better than UAB winning a basketball game so you can see that it is excitement of the highest order. We are so delighted that I would be happy to sign your name, or anyone else's name, to a dinner ticket at Bright Star or Villa Rose or Mauby's or Captain D's or wherever you would like to go. We are ready to celebrate whenever you are rested enough to go someplace and do something. We know that you will be exhausted, physically and emotionally, but will pester you nevertheless to get out and do something as soon as we can.

We are still learning about Lupus and have an appointment with Dr. Boulware (I may have already mentioned this) to get as much info as we can about how to proceed. We are also in the third week of a three week program to get my Achilles tendons to act like they are only about 65 instead of whatever they are. I must get back to six times a week golf so Woowoo can properly supervise the housecleaning and get the cat to behave the way she is supposed to. Besides, she has miles to go before she sleeps, and many promises to keep. Woowoo, this is, not Yumyum. Let me know if you need a scorecard to keep up with these mnemonic like names.

Meal planning has become high adventure. A ham sandwich or a bowl of soup can become epicurious if treated with respect and enough mustard and other seasonings. Today we (editorially speaking, again) are contemplating orange roughy. The tricky part about that is that the recipes on hand are for halibut or salmon, so you have a substitution before you start. On closer inspection, which is a very good way to look at something in a very close way, is to skip the fish and concentrate on the other items like roasted asparagus, minced orange peel, lemon-caper sauce and roasted potatoes. The backup plan is to grill a couple of hot dogs. OR, here is a thought— get John to do that thing with pecans glued to catfish somehow. When those inspirational inspirations happen, it is like a flash of lightning, sometimes referred to in a scholarly sense, as fulgurant. Sounds like something vulgar but perhaps with the right timing and delivery, would be accepted with a minimum of decorum. Do not want to have any more decorum than is necessary to continue down the road of capturing the Huns so we can begin that thing known as civilization before the Romans ruined it by trying to run the whole show and fouled up the civilization thing for several centuries. A classic paragraph that could be entitled "From Fish to Fowl in one fell swoop." I saw a fishhawk swoop and catch a fish a couple of times, but never went from fish to fowl before.

And that's sort of how it was on Sunday, March 11, at 11:15 a.m. We will leave it right there and await further instructions.

dy
everyone is ENTITLED to a struggle

03/11/2001

## don belk young

**From:**     "don belk young"
**To:**       "john downey" <jjones2742@aol.com>
**Sent:**     Monday, March 12, 2001 3:19 PM
**Subject:**  TOLD YOU SO

Even a cursory perusal of back issues would reveal clearly that this pundit stated quite distinctly and without any fear or doubt that UAB would not be doing post season play. And so it came to pass and nothing more needs to be said. So we will not say any more about it unless you have a question. Please refer questions to someone, anyone. We do not want to talk about it other than to say "I told you so."

This day, March 12, 2001, is destined to be relegated to obscurity because it shows little regard for the comfort of those to whom it is host and hostess. Makes one feel more like a hostage than anything else. It would be depressing if we did not have a ban against depression in any form. There have been no redeeming characteristics so far. It seems irresponsible to try to relegate a day when it is an inanimate object and cannot do anything about it, but we were having one of those stream of consciousness days and there it was. Is it better to be relegated than regulated? Yes. We would explain but would not want the readership to be afflicted with MEGO. We might lose them before the first issue comes off the press. We will proceed in the usual way by taking liberty with the language, the subject matter, and whatever else might get in the way.

For about 30 minutes we have been attempting to cut and paste from the clipart program, but have decided that we were not supposed to be able to do that, at least not today. So those pictures (icons) will have to wait until later, perhaps never. Another thing that I have not tried is to send an attachment. Must be easy because some of the email comes with attachments, and some of it can be opened. And some of it cannot be opened. I feel certain that it has something to do with the learning curve, skill level, and attitude. Gotta watch those attitudes.

The highlight of today has not appeared yet. The problem with that is that about all that is left to do is to fix some chicken breasts with cream of mushroom soup for supper; then off to a meeting of the Southlake Townhomes Owners association. The best thing about the meeting is that the host will have angel food cake, strawberries, and fresh coffee, which should help in the never ending battle to stamp out stupidity and uselessness. These traits inevitably present themselves in almost every sentence uttered during the entire meeting. A notable exception would be the report of the Treasurer. It becomes a mind game whereby it is necessary to commit complicity to engage in duplicity, all the while attempting to find simplicity. On the other hand, a plethora could be a good thing if it was called money while a disorganized failure would be better described as a shambles.

Gotta go, so we are gone.

dy
everyone is ENTITLED to a struggle

03/12/2001

# don belk young

**From:** "don belk young"
**To:** "john downey" <jjones2742@aol.com>
**Sent:** Tuesday, March 13, 2001 9:21 AM
**Subject:** BIG DAY IN LITTLE ROCK

We have information from a usually reliable source that this is getaway day, also known as the big day in Little Rock Excitement is probably overcome with fatigue. We sincerely wish for you a restful night in Memphis and a good trip home. And we are ready to help with whatever we can when you are here. My advice. Just do one thing at a time. Or as that famous philosopher, the one who was called lazy and shiftless by his best friends, said "Take your time, all other graces, will follow in their natural places." And you can tell them that I said so, with vigor.

John, your stature has come into question. Woowoo had suggested (ordered) that the kitchen floor be mopped, and remembered that Edith had made a similar request and you opined that it would diminish your stature, but were reminded that whatever you might have had was imaginary, and was further limited by being imagined only in your imagination. In other words, you could not lose something that you never had, despite The allegations of victims worldwide. That provided an opportunity to suggest that neither (that's pronounced with a hard I) of us had ever had any stature in terms of how far we were from the sky when we were standing straight up.

Five score and seven days ago we started originating, editing, spell checking, and mailing daily memos. So we missed an opportunity seven days ago to celebrate the centennial. Surely this occasion should not go uncelebrated. Might as well forget Cinco de Mayo and April Fool's Day. The official day to mark this occasion shall be designated as March 6 and will never be celebrated on Monday, no matter how many Presidents were born on that day.

One of those random thoughts just rushed into today's stream of consciousness. The suggestion was that the frequent use of malapropisms was unintentional, no matter how it was defined. So let me assure you, faithful reader, that any malapropisms used herein was intentional, which converts such events into propisms.

With promises of continued propisms, we will go on temporary leave.

dy
everyone is ENTITLED to a struggle

03/13/2001

## don belk young

| | |
|---|---|
| **From:** | "don belk young" |
| **To:** | "john downey" <jjones2742@aol.com> |
| **Sent:** | Wednesday, March 14, 2001 6:37 PM |
| **Subject:** | IT WAS PROBABLY AN OK DAY |

All in all, after all is said and done, and noting with muted extemporaneousness that the sun did not shine all day, on a scale of ten, the excitement was about 1. That would have to be the fairway shot on no. 16. Would give you a detail report but might not be able to resist an exaggeration or two, so to protect the integrity and preserve the timeliness and thoroughness with which these notes are prepared, will just say that it was spectacular. Should more detail be required, please give ample notice so witnesses can be subpoenaed and a proper forum obtained for them to witness.

It has come to our attention that popocuranation is rapidly obtaining epidemic proportions. My observation is that when an epidemic occurs, it always seems to happen rapidly. And the reason for that can be reasoned by using common sense. Must be careful here not to use the reserves we have in the common sense category. They need to be rationed in a rational way lest they be depleted and we all start behaving without common sense. But enough about common sense and epidemics. Got a little distracted there with those neutron like things bouncing around inside the cranium. Back to pococurante. Prima facie evidence, which by all accounts is the best kind, would lead one to a conclusion. And if you have a conclusion that you need to come to, just say that you arrived there prima facie.

But wait. We not only never did explain the Tallahassee thing, we have not dealt with pococurante. The reason for this is that we are apathetic, uninterested, unworried, indifferent and nonchalantly detached from any concerns about what the hell pococurante is. As that philosopher out there on the edge somewhere has been known to write in a memo dated March 13, 2001, and sent by email at 10:57, and we will quote here "Things are going to get a lot worse before they get worse."

The excitement rating of 1 is subject to revision since the day is not finished, and we are about to embark on a mission to rescue something at the Galleria. That could very easily affect the rating, most likely to the minus column, which some of those who do rankings have been known to do, especially after violating the rules at the wine tasting and actually swallowing the stuff—you are supposed to spit. Disgusting, to say the least. Who would want a wine that a winetaster would spit out.

Louis XIV of France has come to my attention. He was the same age that I am in 1715 and had worked eight hours a day for all of his 72 years as King of France. He left the world no better than he found it and much worse in some respects. He had no friends; he never wanted any. His life shows what can be done with plenty of time and money and hardly any sense. No one can recall a magnificent deed or worthy thought. Louis had to marry Marie-Therese for political reasons. She ate garlic, but so did Louis, so it didn't matter. She also had Hapsburg lip and cried all the time.

We are on our way to Parisian's and will come back when we are good and ready. And don't you forget it unless you want to. We would do the same for you, no questions asked, as they say in most civilized society, whether they have any culture or not.

And that's the way it is, one more time.

dy
everyone is ENTITLED to a struggle


03/14/2001

## don belk young

| | |
|---|---|
| **From:** | "don belk young" <donbelk@bellsouth.net> |
| **To:** | "john downey" <jjones2742@aol.com> |
| **Cc:** | "cynthia" <waruggles@aol.com>; |
| | "sheryl" <sy180@hotmail.com>; |
| | "nona" <nonat@juno.com>; |
| | "geoff/jan young" <tellulah123@aol.com>; |
| | "mark martin" <mhmartin@sass.uab.edu>; |
| | "dinah martin" <dinah42@hotmail.com> |
| **Sent:** | Monday, March 26, 2001 8:39 AM |
| **Subject:** | WOOWOO |

Ten a.m. today Woowoo has a scheduled MRI. Then a discussion with Dr. Hadley, neurosurgeon, about what to do about it. Has had a very painful pinched nerve for several days, about two weeks, along with continuing arthritis symptoms. And Dr. McClain diagnosed lupus, then a few days later Dr. Boulware said he cannot say that she has lupus and that he cannot say that she does not have lupus.

After about a two week leave from daily creativity, seems like a good time to reprise the practice. It may not work because I have never been able to reprise just because I wanted to. Most reprises have been either automatic or axiomatic, and the best part is that you cannot tell the difference. The thing is, if you have a reprise, it's probably better to keep it to yourself. You start talking about it and someone is likely to ask you what it is. A long silence would be the most likely outcome. That might be a good thing, except the party of the other part would assume that your muteness was a sign of idiocy or ignorance or apathy, and would become irate. Then you could turn the whole thing around and inquire about irateness and perhaps achieve a similar beneficial result.

As you must know by now, my stream of consciousness is almost always at work except when I need it. But the business about muteness brings to mind the best feature of computers, TVs, and other similar devices. These are manmade as far as I know, and man has determined that a mute button is a necessary thing on such devices. But man himself, or more accurately herself, does not have a mute button, and, if she did, it would most assuredly be disabled.

I have probably offended nine out of ten female readers, which is an unintended outcome, but as you know, we do not always control the content of these epistles. It just happens.

Do you have the hibiscus of the year 2001 in place? And don't forget the monkey grass!!!!!

dy
everyone is ENTITLED to a struggle

03/26/2001

## don belk young

| | |
|---|---|
| **From:** | "don belk young" <donbelk@bellsouth.net> |
| **To:** | "john downey" <jjones2742@aol.com> |
| **Cc:** | "gloria" <gwalker@uabmc.edu> |
| **Sent:** | Sunday, May 20, 2001 3:19 PM |
| **Subject:** | AN APPROPRIATE SUBJECT WOULD BE SHOWN HERE IF THERE WAS |

John, we want you and Eydie to find a way to get out of Arkansas. And we are sure that you would like to do so. We sure do miss those same old jokes!!!!!

Did you figure out how to Personalize your Platitudes? Probably not. It is one of those things that seems to be a natural characteristic of those of lesser stature so you certainly do not qualify. Perhaps when your stature has increased until you are classified as "lesser" it will become readily available. We shall await your report with unabated breath.

About Gloria Walker Moon's email address. The one I have is gwalker@ uabmc.edu.

Woowoo is making progress in recovering from the surgery. It was called decompression, quite appropriate since the problem was a compressed nerve. Says that she will wear her bikini anyhow and surgical scars be damned. Problem is she never had a bikini; still doesn't.

I survived a trip to Hillsboro, Ill. Drove Mike's Mercedes and it was an exceptional experience driving a car with 177,000 miles on the odometer. Ran like new, as they say. Golf game with brother Frank on Wed. and Thur. Had a score of 94 on Wed and 87 on Thur. Do you suppose that we could have played on Fri. and Sat. and my score would have been 73. NO. Anyhow, we had a good time and our two sisters joined us on Friday night for dinner at the Depot in Vandalia, Ill. Why do you need to know this? You really do not, so just skip the part that you do not want to know about.

You know that we will do anything we can, like go by the house or whatever. We assume that Henry and Michael look around on a regular basis. Nevertheless, let us know if we can do anything.

dy
everyone is ENTITLED to a struggle

05/24/2001

## don belk young

| | |
|---|---|
| **From:** | "don belk young" <donbelk@bellsouth.net> |
| **To:** | "john downey" <jjones2742@aol.com> |
| **Sent:** | Saturday, June 16, 2001 3:11 PM |
| **Subject:** | TO DELIQUESCE WITHOUT BEING MINACIOUS |

The plan is to deliquesce before we finish. But not to do in a minatory manner.

A complete supply of blonde stories have arrived recently. I will improve on the presentation by using one lead-in instead of repeating.

She was sooooooo BLONDE that

she thought a quarterback was a refund; she studied for a blood test; she sold the car for gas money; if she spoke her mind she would be speechless; she thought grape nuts was a venereal disease; she tried to put M&Ms in alphabetical order; she tripped over a cordless phone.

Enough of that. On to the weekly news.

Madeleine was 9 years old on June 8 and I forgot about it. Must deal with that right away.

Spent $1000 on the deck. Have not done anything for 8 years and it is guaranteed to look "as good as new" for ten years. So $1000/18= $55.55 per year. Conclusion: Ok, I guess.

Did something last Thursday that I had never before done, and I have been around long enough to know better. Sold four items of furniture while store sitting at Oak City down thar "round Harpersville somewheres. Then on Friday had three pars in a row at no. 9 10, and 11.

Gene Bartow called yesterday about Barbeque at the Full Moon next Tuesday. When he said that he was buying the lunch, I asked what time I should be there. Dudley could not come—doing some golfing somewhere in Mississippi; Ray demurred, presumably because of Jan, but come to think about it, he may be going to Miss. for golf, also. Said he had not been able to get the mayor of Vestavia Hills or SRH. I was impressed because he was making his own phone calls from home.

(I know that you must know who Madeleine is. She is no. 2 daughter of Cynthia and they now live in a Memphis suburb.)

You will not believe this. Just found the definitions for those teaser words at the beginning. And guess what. They were used perfectly. Because we will now deliquesce, but not do so in a minatory manner.

Let us know how both of you are.

The local restaurateurs are suffering.

dy
everyone is ENTITLED to a struggle

06/16/2001

2000

Dec. 1 OLD RELIABLE

Dec. 5 AND YET ANOTHER

Dec. 13 ETAL

Dec. 13 THIS AND THAT

Dec. 22 PROBLEM WITH COMPUTER

Dec. 23 NO STATIONERY

Dec. 29 CURRENT STATUS


2001

Jan. 1 RESPONDING TO 2001 email message

Jan. 4 GOOD NEWS

Jan. 15 HELLO TO THE YOUNGS

Jan. 19 HELLO DY

Jan. 23 JESSE'S UNWED MOTHERS FUND

Jan. 27 SCHOLARLY DISCOURSE

Jan. 28 DY


Feb. 4

Feb. 10 RE ANOTHER DAY COME AND GONE

Feb. 17 PRESSED

Feb. 22

Feb. 28 HUSBANDS


Mar. 3

Mar. 6 WHAT TIME IS IT

Mar. 10 THE GOOD AND THE NOT-SO
Mar. 13 HOME

Apr. 2 THE ALBINO
Apr. 27
Apr. 28

June 10 ROY KIRKPATRICK
June 12 LATEST DEVELOPMENTS

**don belk young**

| | |
|---|---|
| **From:** | <JJones2742@aol.com> |
| **To:** | <donbelk@bellsouth.net> |
| **Sent:** | Friday, December 01, 2000 5:53 PM |
| **Subject:** | Re: OLD RELIABLE |

Dear Old Reliable,

Thanks for the epistles you have sent to us this week. We have been on a whirlwind the past few days and I have not had time to get it up (the computer that is...or anything else as far as that goes). So, I was able to read all of them at one time in sequence. I hope you are keeping these jewels of wisdom and erudition for posterity.

We received a disappointing report from the test and examinations Eydie had during the past week. Her cancer is back and is aggressive. She was in remission when we were here in September. We never dreamed it would be back so soon.

This means they may have to change the plans for the kind of treatment that will be used. We will know next week just what will be before us. Eydie is handling it well. In fact she and her sister are out shopping as I send this email. Her sister is going to be the donor for the transplant and they are proceeding to harvest her stem cells.

I will keep you informed as we get things settled. Our address here in Little Rock is:

> Turtle Creek Apartment Homes
> 601 Napa Valley - # 813
> Little Rock, Arkansas 72211

Convey our regards to Shirley.

John

12/01/2000

**don belk young**

| | |
|---|---|
| **From:** | \<JJones2742@aol.com\> |
| **To:** | \<donbelk@bellsouth.net\> |
| **Sent:** | Tuesday, December 05, 2000 10:10 AM |
| **Subject:** | Re: AND YET ANOTHER |

This is from the better half of the Jones household, although I'm not sure what's better about it. This is the first a.m. we have had off since arriving—I mean that I have had off (going to the clinic including Sat & Sun). John has been staying here some (working he says, but I'm not sure on what...  ...I think resting......and when I ask......it seems he considers answering emails work....since it takes so much time (he's slow at picking out the keys - not as fast as you (meaning you - Don, not me), he says).

I don't think we should deprive y'all of our routine. This a.m., it was coffee, then tea, and unpacking some things that were still in a bag (my bag - as you know, John is much more organized), John says he is going to make oatmeal, but just discovered we have a package at the office, so has gone to get it. He got up early this a.m. to take Janet to the clinic. This is her second day of "stem cell harvesting." I've not let her drink any wine for the last two nights as I don't want any alcohol in my new bone marrow.

But Janet's and my routine has been struggling to get up in the a.m.......we are not morning people......and wwwwaaaaaiiiiiiittttttttiiiiiiiinnnnnnngggggggggg...  ...in the clinic, or someplace else at the hospital. Even though they postponed the decision as to what and when I will do until tomorrow, we still have things to do at the ACRC every day. Janet is leaving tomorrow morning; I will miss having her here. Some excitement......the package contains shortbread cookies (my favorite Xmas cookie) that Janet and her daughter made......but Janet forgot to bring, so Melissa mailed them.

Please keep the daily news coming from the Young household. If I go into the hospital tomorrow, I'm going to have John bring them so I can have a chuckle at least once a day. I've been saving cartoons for the past five years in preparation for this moment, but they probably will get old after a while.

I don't have a clever sign off, but will have to come up with something. Eydie

12/05/2000

## don belk young

| | |
|---|---|
| **From:** | <JJones2742@aol.com> |
| **To:** | <donbelk@bellsouth.net> |
| **Sent:** | Wednesday, December 13, 2000 7:14 PM |
| **Subject:** | Re: ETAL |

Don,

I think I have a quodlibet for you. As I understand this term it addresses some types of discussion points. My quodlibet for you is......How in the Hell do I retrieve something from you that contains a "Down Load" attachment. I have down loaded ETAL but I cannot get it back up (ETAL that is). Henry will be here Friday. Maybe he can help me. I am able to receive all of your other dissertations. In fact the reason that I cannot retrieve this email message may be that I have had an epiphany.

I just got in from the hospital. Eydie is doing about as well as we could expect. She is now neutropenci (no immune system) but that should be resolved as soon as her sister's stem cells that were infused begin to graft and produce white cells, red cells and platelets.

Today I heard a big explosion coming from the South and East of Little Rock. I decided that it was a rally being held in Birmingham when Gore conceded. Tell Shirley to have a drink for me as you toast this occasion. I am glad to get this over.

Til we meet again.
John

12/14/2000

## don belk young

| | |
|---|---|
| **From:** | <JJones2742@aol.com> |
| **To:** | <donbelk@bellsouth.net> |
| **Sent:** | Wednesday, December 13, 2000 9:41 AM |
| **Subject:** | Re: THIS AND THAT |

Don,

Your latest philosophical discourse was in my opinion your best. Maybe I think so because I could identify with so much of what you said.

The word QUODLIBET is a classic example you are right, I can talk all day without saying anything. Who else do you know that can do that? How do think I survived for 40 years dealing with college students?

I am delighted that we have so many things in common. My brother Jim sounds exactly like your brother Frank. Moreover, my mother was a school teacher for over 50 years and she would react to Jim and I just as your mother did to Frank and you.

The issue that really got my attention was the fact that you had an epiphany yesterday. I am not familiar with this word but the symptoms you described (swollen, itchy, and then went away) sounds to me like one of the first stages of impotency. I believe I would see a urologist if I were you.

The description of your experience in hanging a Christmas wreath outside the front door was very interesting, but contradictory to what I have always thought of your style. How could a man with your impeccable record of financial wizardry NOT COUNT OVERHEAD in the total expense of such an endeavor as this? Especially when over the past quarter century you used overhead finances to support such things at UAB athletics and other important expenditures.

So much for the Bull Shit.

Eydie is still getting along pretty well. She is well enough to talk the nurses on the 7th floor of the hospital to move her to a larger room with a view. She is now in room 780 with a telephone number of 501-614-2780.

How is Shirley getting along following the health problem she had? It is always good to hear from you.

John

12/13/2000

**don belk young**

| | |
|---|---|
| From: | <JJones2742@aol.com> |
| To: | <donbelk@bellsouth.net> |
| Sent: | Friday, December 22, 2000 9:46 AM |
| Subject: | Re: Problem with Computer |

Don.

I have been unable to receive the last several messages you sent. I get the headings but when a "Download" is required, I am unable to retrieve the message after I have downloaded the heading. I have about decided that the problem is one of three things. (1) We have different software in our computers, or (2) We have different companies transmitting the message, or (3) It is because of my stupidity.

It is probably number 3 since, I am a certified (Pigmy of Erudition) regarding computers and many other things too. Michael is coming here Sunday to be with his mother on Christmas. He is my computer guru, and may be able to help me get this problem corrected.

Eydie appreciated Shirley's phone call. It really gave her a lift. She is about the same as she was the last time I communicated with you. It has been 14 days since the transplant and they are expecting her to make some positive changes soon with the low blood cell count she is presently experiencing. I will keep you informed as we know what to expect.

Hope you and your family have a happy holiday season.

John D.

12/22/2000

**don belk young**

| | |
|---|---|
| **From:** | <JJones2742@aol.com> |
| **To:** | <donbelk@bellsouth.net> |
| **Sent:** | Saturday, December 23, 2000 3:57 PM |
| **Subject:** | Re: NO STATIONERY |

Don,

Thanks for your latest epistle. I can't wait to let Eydie read it. It will make her day.

She is getting along about the same as she has the past week or so. The Docs tell us not to worry, she is doing fine. She is going to get a pass to get out of the hospital Christmas Day and come to the apartment for Christmas dinner. Henry is here now and Michael gets in tomorrow.

What a relief it is to know that it was not my stupidity (Pigmy of Erudition) that caused me to be unable to retrieve several of your latest renditions. Your email came through great this time.

Convey our best wishes for a Happy Holiday Season to Shirley.

John

12/23/2000

**don belk young**

| | |
|---|---|
| From: | <JJones2742@aol.com> |
| To: | <donbelk@bellsouth.net> |
| Sent: | Friday, December 29, 2000 5:55 PM |
| Subject: | Re: Current Status |

Don,

Sorry that I have not kept up with my correspondence. Things have been pretty hectic here with the snow, ice, and freezing rain. The city was just about shut down. The hospital cafeteria almost ran out of food, and we lost power at the Turtle Creek Apartments.

All this happened while Henry and Michael were here and we were getting ready to bring Eydie to the apartment for Christmas Day party. Instead, we all had to spend a couple of nights at the hospital, sleeping wherever we could find a horizontal space that would accommodate us (that is all of us but Eydie who had her regular room).

On a more positive note, Eydie's blood counts have begun to rise and if this continues, we may get released from the hospital next week. She will then have to came in daily to the clinic for tests and examinations.

I have followed the weather pattern in the news and it appears that you got a pretty good winter storm there. I guess the bottom line about weather is like Will Rogers said, "Everybody talks about the weather, but nobody does anything about it."

Our best wishes to Shirley. We look forward to being with you again.

John

12/30/2000

## don belk young

| | |
|---|---|
| **From:** | <JJones2742@aol.com> |
| **To:** | <donbelk@bellsouth.net> |
| **Sent:** | Monday, January 01, 2001 12:19 PM |
| **Subject:** | Re: Responding to 2001 E-Mail Message |

Shirley and Don,

Thanks for your 20001 message. It is always a good experience getting you writings. I appreciate you taking time to give us an update on what is going on in Birmingham as well as the scholarly-manner in which you enlighten us on a plethora of subjects. We look forward to hearing from you. I am going to keep these epistles and bind them-for our future enjoyment.

I just got back to the apartment after spending the night at the hospital. Eydie continues to improve physically, but she is worn our emotionally. We watched the new millennium activities on TV in her hospital room and I slept there on a recliner. Her blood counts have improved significantly and she is getting good reports on her heart, kidney, lungs and liver activities. Today the Doc said that he is going to perform a specific type of blood test later this week to determine which of the bone marrow cells are Eydie's and which of them or her sister's. The results of this test will determine the procedures he will use to get everything in order. She may be dismissed from the hospital and move to the apartment the later part of this week.

Thanks for your continues interest and support. HAPPY NEW YEAR!

John

01/01/2001

**don belk young**
_____

From:             &lt;JJones2742@aol.com&gt;
To:               &lt;donbelk@bellsouth.net&gt;
Sent:             Thursday, January 04, 2001 7:46 PM
Subject:          Re: GOOD NEWS!!!!!

Don,

I just returned from the hospital after being there all day. We were delighted to have the Doc in charge tell us that Eydie's blood counts have stabilized and that the graft of her sister's cells has been confirmed. She will be discharged from the hospital tomorrow and will come to the apartment we have leased here in Little Rock. She will be followed as an outpatient on a daily basis for a couple of months. if every continues to go the way that it has we will then be able to return home.

Your epistles have kept me from going crazy over the past month or so. The latest of them required me to carefully examine then more than once before I could respond. I do have a few questions and comments. They are:

1. If the cousin of obtuse is otiose, what is the relationship between obtuse and adios (like in "Adios Amigo," that is Spanish for "Goodbye Friend")?

2. I agree with anonymous that "No one should grow old who isn't prepared to be ridiculous," but I would add to this a phrase "and to take a vow of celibacy."

3. In your rendition of 1/4/2001, you concluded with a charge to fill in the blank with an eight letter word. I would like to submit the following suggestion. "Everyone is entitled to a whipping." This is based on the philosophy of my maternal Grandmother who descended from German ancestry, The Von

der Bergs of Northern Prussia, who believed very strongly the
if "You spare the rod, you spoil the child."

Our Best to Shirley. We are looking forwarding to being with you again,

John D

01/05/2001

| From: | <JJones2742@aol.com> |
| To: | <donbelk@bellsouth.net> |
| Sent: | Monday, January 15, 2001 8:42 AM |
| Subject: | Re: |

"Hello" To The Youngs,

There is not much to report from Arkansas. It's still cold here and there's not much change in Eydie's condition. As you are aware she was discharged from the hospital, but the term "Discharged" is a misnomer. She spends as much time as she ever did in the hospital except she must return home at night. And, yes it is night before we can get home. By that time we are both exhausted.

Well, enough whining. In that case, think I will demur from whining and became more sanguine.

Even though Eydie's blood counts are slow about returning to normal, we are being told that this is a normal situation following one of these type transplants. Her appetite has returned and she is basically feeling pretty good.

It looks like the Blazers are in for a rough season. I regret it for Murray's sake. I have known him since he was a small kid and have always admired him.

Well, I guess I better go start and warm up the car. Miss Eydie will have to leave here in a few minutes if she is going to make her appointment at the hospital on time (which she has never been able to do).

Our best wishes to the "YOUNG CLAN." Will keep in touch.

John

01/15/2001

## don belk young

| | |
|---|---|
| **From:** | <JJones2742@aol.com> |
| **To:** | <donbelk@bellsouth.net> |
| **Sent:** | Friday, January 19, 2001 8:41 AM |
| **Subject:** | Re: |

HELLO DY,

John asked me to write something that he could type and send to you in the morning. You see since chemo has damaged my short term memory, he has had to use his supplemental erudition to help keep my appointments, meds., etc., in order. (Ed. Note: that is in addition to grocery shopping, cooking, washing dishes, cleaning bathrooms, mopping floors, paying bills, running errands, and above all "Driving Miss Eydie." ...Yes, with these arrangements, the typist has some editorial privileges) Therefore, his intellectual capacity to respond to the mental challenges of The Young Newsletter was not there...as in nowhere to be found.

Well, I mentally composed a couple of paragraphs in my head and thought, "surely I'll remember them in the morning." But...another voice said, "No... you better write it now and leave it for him to type and send in the morning." Would you believe, by then I had already forgotten my first paragraph!

Anyway, remember the boy/pony story where the boy is digging in the manure and says, "with all this s-- (you fill in the four letter word) there's got to be a pony in were somewhere! Well, my "pony" has been losing 10 pounds during the past couple of months. But...I've discovered yet another pony. You are, however, going to had to wait for another Jones Bulletin for the answer to be revealed.

"Hi" to Woo Woo and please pass on to her that I will not know the news of the bone marrow aspiration I had last Friday by today as expected. The individual who wrote the order neglected to check the test that was needed regarding my sisters bone marrow engraftment. The Doctor apologized, but it didn't make my day. He now wants to wait until Day 60 which will be sometime in February since I had three bone marrows in one month. I believe I'll be contented to wait.

EJ
Assistant Editor

01/19/2001

## don belk young

| | |
|---|---|
| **From:** | <shargrove@fairview.buncombe.k12.nc.us> |
| **To:** | <layfield@nis.k12.la.us>; |
| | <dfordham@pineynet.com>; |
| | <mcornelius@alggraphics.com>; |
| | <JJones2742@aol.com>; |
| | <ehplott@home.com> |
| **Sent:** | Friday, January 19, 2001 6:48 AM |
| **Subject:** | Jesse's Unwed Mother's Fund |

Dear Bros and Sisters,

Due to circumstances beyond my control—it is George W.'s fault—I be needing some cash and I need yo help. Please send yo money to Jesse's Unwed Mother's Fund or I Be Messing Around Fund as soon as you can. It is the Right Wing's fault. Just remember, I be yo spiritual leader. Look forward to getting yo money.

Love,
Rev. Jesse

01/23/2001

**don belk young**

| | |
|---|---|
| **From:** | <JJones2742@aol.com> |
| **To:** | <donbelk@bellsouth.net> |
| **Sent:** | Tuesday, January 23, 2001 6:50 PM |
| **Attach:** | ATT00007.eml |
| **Subject:** | Fwd: Jesse's Unwed Mother's Fund |

DY - You have some competition in the creative writing department. It appears, however, that he is not quite as erudite as you are.

Regarding your last epistle, John has proclaimed that among other things, the road to hell is paved with good intentions.

The patient.

P.S. As W.C. said "Never, Never, Never, Never, Never GIVE UP!"

01/23/2001

## don belk young

| | |
|---|---|
| **From:** | <JJones2742@aol.com> |
| **To:** | <donbelk@bellsouth.net> |
| **Sent:** | Saturday, January 27, 2001 12:55 PM |
| **Subject:** | Re: INTELLECTUAL DISCOURSE |

DY,

I regret that time has not permitted to respond to each of your masterpieces of literary genus. This is the first day that we have not had to go in to the Hospital and spend hours doing whatever.

Yesterday They gave Eydie a "Stem Cell Boost," which is another way of saying another infusion of her sisters blood. They are walking a fine line to (1) maintain a balance between getting a good engraftment from her sister's cells and (2) impeding the development of Graft Vs Host disease as her sisters T cells attack various organs within Eydie' body as if they are foreign bodies.

Overall, she seems to be progressing pretty well. Most of her blood counts are in good shape and she is talking about going shopping...So, this is a good sign.

Now to the intellectual discourse. I am amazed to read the broad array of topics which you have mastered. We have discussed going down to the Barnes and Noble Bookstore, that is only a few blocks from where we live, and purchase a Thesaurus. We did not bring ours, nor did we bring a dictionary. I will attempt to respond to some of your topics based on my perception of whet think you are discussing.

The first one that caught my attention is "CLEEK." You mentioned that you had one, but was never aware of it until now. My first thought is that there may be a typographic error and you mean 'CREEK.' If this be the case I am quite conformable with this term in that It was the place that I learned to swim. I can remember it well. The warm sunny days with all little kids in the water naked with the big "Bank Walkers" strolling around on the creek banks.

The next subject addresses languages. I have studied French (Parlez-vous Français...Do you speak French) or Vous Les Vous Couchez Avec Moi (will you sleep with me); but I have never mastered Argot.

I can hardly wait for the arrival of Waitangi Day. I assume that this day is similar to Waitonya. Day Which is the one day during the year that a man doesn't have to wait for thirty minutes on his wife to get ready to go somewhere.

Finally, I am unable to identify with receiving a "Short Shrift." Are you sure you don't mean receiving a short "shaft"? Or, in the college dormitories and in military barracks there are times one would act "Short Sheeted."

In any event, I am looking forward to learning more about Tallahassee and Halliday.

Our best to Shirley. We are planning to watch the UAB/Memphis game on television tonight. We will be looking for you in the crowd.

Yours in the Spirit of Erudition,

JDJ

01/27/2001

## don belk young

| From: | <JJones2742@aol.com> |
|---|---|
| To: | <donbelk@bellsouth.net> |
| Sent: | Sunday, January 28, 2001 9:17 PM |
| Subject: | Re: |

DY,

Just another day today. We spent a considerable amount of time at the hospital, but received a good report, so that make the mission worthwhile. Eydie's blood counts and kidney markers are getting closer to normal; which is a good sign.

Last night we watched the Blazers on TV and agonized with the rest of the UAB fans. Eydie really got caught up in the game especially in the second half. I heard her use some words I seldom hear her utter. They were four letter expletives. I did not know if she was telling me she wanted me to take her to bed, or is she was saying that she needed to go to the bathroom. If you quote me on this, I will deny it.

The Blazers reminded me of an old saying. That is that something or someone "Went Down Like a One Egg Puddin." I guess that was a way of saying "They went flat." This was especially true during the overtime.

We looked for you and Shirley every time the cameras panned the crowd, but to no avail.

Tomorrow is another day. We are due at the hospital at 9:00 A.M. for further exams and tests. Will try to keep you informed as changes occur.

Eydie and I reached an unanimous decision (unlike the Supreme Court's decision regarding the presidential election) that your scholarly renditions place you in the same company as true scholars (i.e., Robert P. Glaze and others). I am, however, still waiting to know about the origination of Tallahassee and Halliday.

On a serious note, thanks for your interest and support.

JDJ

01/29/2001

## don belk young

**From:**      <JJones2742@aol.com>
**To:**        <donbelk@bellsouth.net>
**Sent:**      Sunday, February 04, 2001 11:18 AM
**Subject:**   Re:

Don,

Our lack of response to your scholarly renditions is in no an indication of our pleasure from getting them. We have each one of your chronicles stored and will someday see if I can get Monica Lewinsky to write a preface to them, and then look for a publisher. If we are successful, you could become a billionaire.

Eydie is slowly gaining strength every day. Some of her blood counts are still slow about returning to normal, but others are O.K. The greatest problem now is the effect of the medication on her kidneys. They are working on this and hope to get it under control next week. We are still having to return to the hospital every day for tests and examinations.

We watched the Blazers beat So. Miss. yesterday. I was very impressed with their playing. In fact I do not recall many times that they were able to put two halves together like they did against So. Miss. As a matter of record I want to mention that Edyie's control of her language was significantly improved from the Memphis game.

I did not know that Michael had moved his store out east between Chelsea and Harpersville. I am sure it is much safer there. Hope all works out well. He is very fortunate to have you to help him when emergencies arise.

We were impressed that the management of Villa Rosa had the good intelligence to use you and Woowoo for an advertising plan. If you can send us a copy of the picture we would like to see it If you can send it my email, I could print it on my color printer (I think).

I had heard about the fellow who had a craving for barley sugar, but had forgotten that his name was Halliday.

I enjoyed your limericks about the "Three Legged Stool," and the one you want for your epitaph. I believe you termed it "A Couplet." In any event it could be an epitaph for many of us, because......Life IS a joke and ALL things show it; I thought so once, but now know it."

Our best to Shirley,

John

02/05/2001

## don belk young

| | |
|---|---|
| **From:** | <JJones2742@aol.com> |
| **To:** | <donbelk@bellsouth.net> |
| **Sent:** | Saturday, February 10, 2001 12:48 PM |
| **Subject:** | Re: ANOTHER WEEK COME AND GONE |

DY

It has been difficult for me to keep up with time. Days and weeks seem to go by with a "bat of the eye." It has been 12 weeks since we left home on this journey, but it only seems like a few days. It's really hard to believe that we are now at Day 63 since the transplant. Eydie seems to be improving each day and if this continues they will start figuring out when we may be able to return to Birmingham.

Your daily "Epistles" keep us going, even though I have to read some sentences twice to understand them. The following statements reflect my thoughts about some of your last week's renditions.

1.  Your public statement by the Rev. Jesse Jackson was well received by friends with whom I have shared it. in each case I reminded my friend that this may be something with which he may identify.

2.  You espoused that "The best way to get some, talent that is, is to work for it," I suggest that this proclamation could pertain to things other than talent.

3.  You again referred to the term "Waitangi Day," I keep getting this confused with "Waitonya Day" but I will go back and re-read your correspondence that initiated this subject.

4.  You left me wondering about what the darts had to say about

your troding amok them. I guess you did clarify this somewhat when in a later epistle you defined darts as mud on your shoes or something like that.

5. Your mentioning The Festival of Aphrodite really brought back some of my memories during that period of the late 30's. I also slipped under the tent at a carnival in Monticello, Arkansas to get my first look at a nude woman. My cousin held the tent up for me to get in

6. I am not sure a "Missed Opportunity" is always bad. There have been times that I wish that I had missed the opportunity to do some things I did.

We are getting ready to watch the Blazers play South Florida on TV. I hope the play as well as they did against Southern Mississippi. However, I guess the quality of your opponent has something to do with how well you play.

Our best to Woowoo. We are counting the days until we can get home again.

JDJ

02/11/2001

# don belk young

| | |
|---|---|
| **From:** | \<JJones2742@aol.com\> |
| **To:** | \<donbelk@bellsouth.net\> |
| **Sent:** | Saturday, February 17, 2001 7:10 |
| **Subject:** | Re: PRESSED |

DY,

Sorry to be so slow in responding to your theses. This past week has been very demanding on us. Yesterday Eydie had another transplant of her sister's cells. The first transplant did O.K. for a while, but did not totally graft and replace Eydie's bone marrow. Test this week revealed that her current marrow is composed of 78% donor cells and 28% Eydie cells. For the transplant to be totally successful, the bone marrow must be 100% donor cells. The Docs tell us that this procedure is not uncommon. However, it will require that we remain here for a few more weeks.

Your emails keep us going. I was particularly impressed by your mentioning the curlew. Even though Birmingham is a little too far south for these creatures, I do think I saw one in my back yard last year during the season when the native birds from the Northern Regions of North America go south for the winter.

I also heard about the woodpecker and the redwoods. I think you and I can identify with him.

And, if you should ever run out of Attaboys, I would loan you one of mine. I think that in the early stages of this phenomena, you and Jerry forget that the other one had sent an atta boy to me.

Please convey our best wishes to your Board of Overseers.

JDJ

02/18/2001

From: &lt;JJones2742@aol.com&gt;
To: &lt;donbelk@bellsouth.net&gt;
Sent: Thursday, February 22, 2001 4:38
Subject: Re:

D Y,

Things are about the same here. It seems that every minute of the day is consumed. Eydie is still going into the hospital and regularly having some kind of test done. The rest of the time she is putting me to the test.

In reviewing your "Masterpieces," I came upon a statement you made about "Keeping up with the Joneses." An old friend of mine has a response to that saying. He insists that "You cannot keep up with the Joneses. When you are about to catch up with them, they refinance and go buy something else every time."

We haven't been able to keep up with The Blazers very well. The Arkansas papers and The USA Today do not give us much help. I have been trying to find out how the South Florida (or was it West Florida) game came out. (yes I know that a sentence should never be finished with a preposition or with a proposition). I hope you consumed enough food at the Green and Gold Room for both of us.

What is the latest regarding Jan Boothe? I don't suppose they can be contacted by email can they? I have their mailing address but not their zip code number, but probably (where have I come across that word lately) could get it from the local post office.

Did you ever get the riddle Eydie tried to forward to you? We have exhausted our intellectual abilities trying to figure out the answer. Of course that did not take too much time.

I really do want to have your rendition of "Professor Twist." I have exhausted my three stories and two limericks and need some more material.

Hope all is well with Woowoo. We surely are looking forward to corning home. Remember...NOT EVERYONE is ENTITLED to a struggle.

JDJ

02/23/2001

## don belk young

| | |
|---|---|
| **From:** | <JJones2742@aol.com> |
| **To:** | <donbelk@bellsouth.net> |
| **Sent:** | Wednesday, February 28, 2001 10:18 |
| **Subject:** | Husband's |

We enjoyed the mail yesterday. I can identify with it, but not as well as John - due to age difference, you know.

I can't take credit for this, but thought it was an interesting definition:

"A husband is someone who takes out the trash and tries to give the impression that he just cleaned the whole house." Also I have a joke - hear hear! Since I'm not an author, It's too long to type, but if you can remember the word "parrot" - perhaps I will remember the rest. The chemo this time has really done a number on my short-term memory. I told John today that if we could put both our brains together, we would have a whole person. He questioned that.

John doesn't think he has emailed you this week so I will let you know my good news—I hope. I will have blood sent this Friday for test that will dictate whether or not we can leave weekend after this (March 10). Also will depend on whether or not I have graft vs. host. I can stay in B'ham for two wks. & be followed at UAB, then return to Little Rock for tests & come back monthly thereafter. Let's go to - LaDoce Vita - you know what I mean. I asked the dr. Monday if I can eat out yet & he said if I sit in a corner at least it's out.

Good night!
EMGCJ

03/01/2001

## don belk young

| | |
|---|---|
| **From:** | <JJones2742@aol.com> |
| **To:** | <donbelk@bellsouth.net> |
| **Sent:** | Saturday, March 03, 2001 10:49 |
| **Attach:** | ATT00020.eml |
| **Subject:** | Fwd: |

Don,

I just received the attachment from my son in law. You may have already seen it. It does, however have some very interesting information.

Yesterday Eydie had a blood test that will determine what percentage of her blood cells are her original ones, and what percentage of them are her sisters who was the donor for the transplant. The last time this was done several weeks ago the results were 17% Eydie's original and 83% Janet's donor cells. They want this ratio to finally get to where they are at least 99% Janet's. We will find out the results of this latest test next Friday (March 9) when we have an appointment with the Lead Doc in charge of Allogeneic Transplants.

We are really sorry to miss Bartow's reception last night and the home basketball game with St. Louis tonight. Please represent me well at the buffet in The Green and Gold Room and convey our best to our friends...both of them.

On a final note, I detected from your recent email that your picture is located on the Arena concourse wall. If that is true I am pleased. Without your assistance the UAB athletic program could not have survived in the beginning. However, there are some people who do not realize what an impact you had. One of these persons is Congressman Dan Burton from Indiana. I hope he does not hear of your recognition for this or he may want to hold hearings and demand all the University's financial records from that era. That may be a serious problem for many of us.

It may be true that "Everyone is Entitled to a Struggle" for we have had ours over the past five years and are now ready to graduate.

Our best to Shirley!!!

John

03/03/2001

Page 1 of 1

**don belk young**

| | |
|---|---|
| **From:** | <JJones2742@aol.com> |
| **To:** | <donbelk@bellsouth.net> |
| **Sent:** | Tuesday, March 06, 2001 5:13 |
| **Subject:** | Re: WHAT TIME IS IT |

DY,

We are really eager to hear more about Shirley's diagnosis with LUPUS. I do not know much about this disease but am now going to do research on it. Lil Fahy's daughter was diagnosed with this several years ago. The last I heard she was doing well. Please let us know more about this as you learn more.

Regarding your essays, you are not going to believe it, but I was rolling around in the bed trying to go to sleep the other night and started thinking how these masterpieces could be organized in a publication. I was thinking about organizing them according to some basic categories such as (A) Current News from The Home Front, (B) witticisms, (C) Echoes From the Heart, etc. Of course there would first have to be a PREFACE explaining the context in which these epistles were written. Then it would be necessary to have an INDEX defining all of the words you used that most men and no women had ever heard.

However, after reading your proclamation entitled VICISSITUDES, I tend to agree that they should be organized according to the DATE and TITLE. The TABLE OF CONTENTS could have a few sentences about each one as you suggested. I am sincere about following up on this project.

We are looking forward to Friday with much anticipation. That is the day we see the Head Doc who is over Allogeneic Transplants. We hope to be coming home for a brief period, but if that is not possible we will have to take it in stride.

Please convey our best wishes to Shirley.

JDJ

03/07/2001

## don belk young

| | |
|---|---|
| **From:** | \<JJones2742@aol.com\> |
| **To:** | \<donbelk@bellsouth.net\> |
| **Sent:** | Saturday, March 10, 2001 5:42 PM |
| **Subject:** | Re: THE GOOD AND THE NOT- SO- |

DY,

The good news is that Eydie is in complete remission. There is no trace of cancer cells in her bone marrow, blood, or urine. The not-so-good news is that we will not be able to come home this week end.

The Head Doc wants to review the results of a bone marrow aspiration to determine exactly what the very latest chimerism level is. This reveals the ratio between The number of Eydie's cells and the donors cells that make up her current bone marrow. The outcome of this will determine how they will plan future treatment procedures.

We are scheduled to discuss this with him Tuesday, March 13 at 3:15 p.m. This means that we will probably spend Wednesday the 14th packing, disconnecting the computer, attending to business matters, (i.e. getting the rental furniture picked up, canceling the TV cable and electricity, etc.). Our plans are to drive to Memphis Thursday, spend the evening with my daughter, and come on home Friday the 16th.

We will keep in touch regarding our plans. Hope things are going well at the Young Household. Our best wishes to Woo Woo. Please express to her our thanks for sending the Gene Bartow Reception and Sculpture Unveiling Program.

JDJ

03/11/2001

## don belk young

| | |
|---|---|
| **From:** | <JJones2742@aol.com> |
| **To:** | <donbelk@bellsouth.net> |
| **Sent:** | Tuesday, March 13, 2001 10:57 |
| **Subject:** | Home |

We have a one day delay. Had planned to pack and drive out tomorrow, but the doctor wants me to have a CT scan tomorrow & pick up a letter from him Thursday morning. So the new plan is to leave for Memphis Thurs P.M. and on to B'ham Friday. So …you have one more day to challenge us mentally—if you so choose and are so inclined.

These quotes from women are for WooWoo (she will understand them): Whatever women must do they must do twice as well as men to be thought half as good. Luckily, this is not difficult.

I refuse to think of them as chin hairs. I think of them as stray eyebrows.

A male gynecologist is like an auto mechanic who never owned a car

Old age ain't no place for sissies

Things are going to get a lot worse before they get worse

Things only Women Understand:
Why it's good to have five pairs of black shoes
The difference between cream, ivory, and off-white
FAT CLOTHES
A salad, diet drink, and a hot fudge sundae make a balanced lunch

**don belk young**

| | |
|---|---|
| From: | <JJones2742@aol.com> |
| To: | <donbelk@bellsouth.net> |
| Sent: | Monday, April 02, 2001 9:30 |
| Attach: | ATT00009.eml |
| Subject: | Fwd: The Albino |

DY

Thanks for the April's Fool Card. I tried to send a card back to you but couldn't get my computer to help me get the mission accomplished.

If I can get my income tax project completed this week, I am going to start my next project called The Epistles from Don. Now, this title may cause different people to interpret these writings to be the work of different individuals. Some may think they are the work of Don Juan, the famous Spanish horseman. Others may think that the epistles are from The Don of the Giovanni Family. Then there may even be others, who may have dabbled in the history and philosophy of Higher Education, that might think that the epistles are the work of a 13th century university administrator. The title of "Dean" that is used today in higher education is a derivative of the word "Don" that was used to identify the "Top Dog" at Oxford, Cambridge, Salamanca, Bologna, and The University of Paris, the five cornerstones that formed the foundation of modern higher education as we know it.

We will just have to see how it goes.

Hope Shirley is better. We send our best wishes.

JDJ

04/03/2001

## don belk young

| | |
|---|---|
| **From:** | <JJones2742@aol.com> |
| **To:** | <donbelk@bellsouth.net> |
| **Sent:** | Friday, April 27, 2001 12:45 PM |
| **Subject:** | Re: |

DY,

We had no idea that we were going to be here in Little Rock this long. I did not bring my computer and have been lost without it.

Yesterday I stumbled up on a computer I can use in the family waiting room here in the hospital. It is an old one, very slow, and does not have a printer attached to it. Today I waited in line to use it and figure out how to pull up my email and respond.

Eydie is progressing slowly. She was very sick for several days, She asked me to let you and Shirley know that she has changed rooms here in the hospital and now has a different telephone number. The number in her room is now 501-614-2781.

We are hoping to be able to return home next week sometime.

Hope Shirley is recovering well from her surgery.

John D.

04/27/2001

## don belk young

| | |
|---|---|
| **From:** | <JJones2742@aol.com> |
| **To:** | <donbelk@bellsouth.net> |
| **Sent:** | Saturday, April 28, 2001 1:26 PM |
| **Subject:** | Re: |

Hello - John brought me to the family room today to ck some emails I have received. To explain - I have graft vs. host, which can occur when my sister's cells attack my body. They want some of it, but mine has gone crazy. My dr. wants to leave me on current meds one more day & if doesn't work, will try something else. Hope WooWoo is doing better than when I last talked with her. I've had my struggle, and I'm ready for some non-struggle. Hope to see y'all soon. John or I will keep you updated as computer access permits.

EMG

04/28/2001

## don belk young

| | |
|---|---|
| **From:** | <JJones2742@aol.com> |
| **To:** | <donbelk@bellsouth.net> |
| **Sent:** | Sunday, June 10, 2001 10:56 |
| **Subject:** | Re: ROY KIRKPATRICK |

Don,

Thanks for sending me some details about Roy's family's wishes regarding where they would like memorials sent. Eydie and I have agreed that we want to make a memorial contribution to the American Cancer Society (or whatever the official name is.) I have done this on previous occasions, but do not recall where I sent the check. I do remember that I sent it to an office in Birmingham that is Alabama's Office of the National Organization.

I think the address of the office is in the Birmingham telephone directory. If you can get the address and official name of the organization to which I should send the check, and email it to me, I will go on now and get this done. If it is too much of a hassle, I will just wait until we get home to take care of this.

The only problem is that we do not have a clue as to when we may be coming home. Eydie has been very sick the last two days. She has some kind of blockage in her small intestines or her colon that is reaching the danger point. They have turned her over to the Gastrointestinal docs and the surgeons who are monitoring her closely day and night. We hope that they can resolve this dilemma soon.

I will keep you informed as developments occur.

Swing Parallel with the Flight of the Baseball!!!

JDJ

06/11/2001

## don belk young

**From:** &lt;JJones2742@aol.com&gt;
**To:** &lt;donbelk@bellsouth.net&gt;
**Sent:** Tuesday, June 12, 2001 414
**Subject:** Latest Developments

DY,

We really had a scare this week. The docs had determined that the problem Eydie was having with her intestinal track was going the require surgery. They had diagnosed the problem as a blockage in the colon. However, after more X-Rays, CT Scans, and other tests, it was agreed by all the docs that the blockage was caused by an illuis of the colon and this is treatable.

They have now started treatment for the illuis of the colon and Eydie is beginning to respond.

You can imagine how relieved we were. With Eydie's current weakened condition caused by heavy chemotherapy and large doses of steroids, she may have a difficult time surviving major surgery.

We still do not know when to count on being able to return home. Hope all is well with the Youngs.

JDJ

06/12/2001

## THE POWER OF EPISTLES

Definitions of selected words.

Apodictic–indisputably true

bonnyclabber–thick, soured milk eaten with cream and sugar, honey or molasses

borborygmus–stomach rumble; rumbling sounds made by the movement of gases in the stomach and intestines

clerihew–a humorous or satirical verse consisting of two rhyming couplets in lines of irregular meter about somebody who is named in the verse

crumhorn–a wind instrument of the Renaissance with a curving tube and a double reed

deliquesce–to melt away or disappear

digastric–describes a muscle, especially the muscle on either side of the lower jaw, in which two fleshy parts are connected by a tendon

digerati–people with expertise in computers, the Internet or WWW

kumiss–fermented milk drink; sour tasting milk from a mare or camel

minacious–of a menacing or threatening nature

nasion–the point in the skull where the nasal and frontal bones unite

namaste–honoring that which is sacred

pellucid–transparently clear in style or meaning

psephology–the study of political elections

quodlibet–a theological or philosophical issue presented for formal argument or disputation

revanche–the act of retaliating; revenge

rodomontade–pretentious boasting or bragging, bluster

john downey
don young donbelk@uab.campuscw.net
THE UNTOLD GREEK CLASSIC

Socrates had been teaching his classes under the same shade tree for about a quarter of a century. Philosophically he was quite satisfied with the results of his teaching and did not pay much attention to the tree except to comment on its qualities to demonstrate a point during a lecture or a discussion. But the faculty and most of the students began to lobby for a new tree. After several years of increasing pressure from the faculty, both of them, Socrates decided to request funding for a new tree in his next budget request. The Dean had told him to make do with the old tree, but the pressure was creating so many distractions that he decided to see what could be done about it and went directly to the CMC (Chief Money Changer). The CMC listened patiently.

CMC: How many students in your class this year?

Socrates: We have 27 full time students, sometimes a passerby will stop for a short time and participate while playing a game of chess.

CMC: How much will a new tree cost?

Socrates: One of my students has an uncle who has a tree farm. I believe that we could get a tree for a fair price, maybe 99 dinars.

CMC: We cannot possibly pay for such a tree in the current budget. But perhaps we can work it out. Would your students be willing to pay a small tree fee each year forever? You do understand that once a fee is established it will never be revoked.

Socrates: We would have more current funding but Plato does not pay any fees currently and he most certainly would not pay the tree fee. He is erudite, besides being smart and intelligent. I mean, he can really shoot the bull with the best of them. I am training him to take my place when they bring the hemlock. He would most likely not participate in our intellectual discussions to avoid the tree fee.

CMC: So you have provided for the continuation of your valuable teaching in order to benefit future generations for the next several thousand years. If we amortize the cost of the tree over, say, 200 years, the annual cost per student, without any contribution from Plato, will be affordable by all. We will collect the tree fee beginning with the next term. You can work out the details with the purchasing department any time after October 1. Tell Plato that he will be exempted from this tree fee as long as he participates regularly in your discussions.

Socrates: Oh, wise one, I was certain that you would find a way. On behalf of Plato and all present and future students please accept our sincere thanks and heartfelt gratitude. Is your real name Don Young or John Jones? I know of no others with the intellectual capacity to implement such a brilliant plan. Thank you so much.

And so it came to pass that the system of financing higher education was put in place and continues to provide for the needs of faculty and students, regardless of tenure (hemlock is no longer a factor), curriculum changes and the semester system.